The minimum wage

DATE DUE

OCT 0 2 2014			
OCT 1 8 2017			

The Minimum Wage

Other Books of Related Interest:

Opposing Viewpoints

At Issue

Current Controversies

Issues That Concern You

> "Congress shall make no law … abridging the freedom of speech, or of the press."

First Amendment to the US Constitution

The basic foundation of our democracy is the First Amendment guarantee of freedom of expression. The Opposing Viewpoints series is dedicated to the concept of this basic freedom and the idea that it is more important to practice it than to enshrine it.

OPPOSING
VIEWPOINTS®
SERIES

The Minimum Wage

Noah Berlatsky, Book Editor

GREENHAVEN PRESS
A part of Gale, Cengage Learning

GALE
CENGAGE Learning·

Detroit • New York • San Francisco • New Haven, Conn • Waterville, Maine • London

Elizabeth Des Chenes, *Managing Editor*

© 2012 Greenhaven Press, a part of Gale, Cengage Learning

Gale and Greenhaven Press are registered trademarks used herein under license.

For more information, contact:
Greenhaven Press
27500 Drake Rd.
Farmington Hills, MI 48331-3535
Or you can visit our Internet site at gale.cengage.com.

For product information and technology assistance, contact us at:

Gale Customer Support, 1-800-877-4253.
For permission to use material from this text or product, submit all requests online at www.cengage.com/permissions.

Further permissions questions can be emailed to permissionrequest@cengage.com.

Articles in Greenhaven Press anthologies are often edited for length to meet page requirements. In addition, original titles of these works are changed to clearly present the main thesis and to explicitly indicate the author's opinion. Every effort is made to ensure the Greenhaven Press accurately reflects the original intent of the authors. Every effort has been made to trace the owners of copyrighted material.

Cover images copyright © PaulPaladin/Shutterstock.com, copyright © Jo Lomark/Shutterstock .com, and copyright © Jay Crihfield/Shutterstock.com.

LIBRARY OF CONGRESS CATALOGING-IN-PUBLICATION DATA

The minimum wage / Noah Berlatsky, book editor.
   p. cm. -- (Opposing viewpoints)
  Includes bibliographical references and index.
  ISBN 978-0-7377-5741-5 (hardcover) -- ISBN 978-0-7377-5742-2 (pbk.)
  1. Minimum wage--United States. 2. Minimum wage. I. Berlatsky, Noah.
  HD4918.M59 2012
  331.2'30973--dc23

                                           2011031457

Printed in the United States of America
1 2 3 4 5 6 7 16 15 14 13 12

Contents

Chapter 3: How Does the Minimum Wage Affect Immigration?

Chapter 4: What Are the Issues Surrounding the Minimum Wage in Other Countries?

Why Consider Opposing Viewpoints?

> "The only way in which a human being
> can make some approach to knowing
> the whole of a subject is by hearing
> what can be said about it by persons of
> every variety of opinion and studying
> all modes in which it can be looked at
> by every character of mind. No wise
> man ever acquired his wisdom in any
> mode but this."
>
> *John Stuart Mill*

In our media-intensive culture it is not difficult to find differing opinions. Thousands of newspapers and magazines and dozens of radio and television talk shows resound with differing points of view. The difficulty lies in deciding which opinion to agree with and which "experts" seem the most credible. The more inundated we become with differing opinions and claims, the more essential it is to hone critical reading and thinking skills to evaluate these ideas. Opposing Viewpoints books address this problem directly by presenting stimulating debates that can be used to enhance and teach these skills. The varied opinions contained in each book examine many different aspects of a single issue. While examining these conveniently edited opposing views, readers can develop critical thinking skills such as the ability to compare and contrast authors' credibility, facts, argumentation styles, use of persuasive techniques, and other stylistic tools. In short, the Opposing Viewpoints Series is an ideal way to attain the higher-level thinking and reading skills so essential in a culture of diverse and contradictory opinions.

In addition to providing a tool for critical thinking, Opposing Viewpoints books challenge readers to question their own strongly held opinions and assumptions. Most people form their opinions on the basis of upbringing, peer pressure, and personal, cultural, or professional bias. By reading carefully balanced opposing views, readers must directly confront new ideas as well as the opinions of those with whom they disagree. This is not to argue simplistically that everyone who reads opposing views will—or should—change his or her opinion. Instead, the series enhances readers' understanding of their own views by encouraging confrontation with opposing ideas. Careful examination of others' views can lead to the readers' understanding of the logical inconsistencies in their own opinions, perspective on why they hold an opinion, and the consideration of the possibility that their opinion requires further evaluation.

Evaluating Other Opinions

To ensure that this type of examination occurs, Opposing Viewpoints books present all types of opinions. Prominent spokespeople on different sides of each issue as well as well-known professionals from many disciplines challenge the reader. An additional goal of the series is to provide a forum for other, less known, or even unpopular viewpoints. The opinion of an ordinary person who has had to make the decision to cut off life support from a terminally ill relative, for example, may be just as valuable and provide just as much insight as a medical ethicist's professional opinion. The editors have two additional purposes in including these less known views. One, the editors encourage readers to respect others' opinions—even when not enhanced by professional credibility. It is only by reading or listening to and objectively evaluating others' ideas that one can determine whether they are worthy of consideration. Two, the inclusion of such viewpoints encourages the important critical thinking skill of objectively evaluating an author's credentials and bias. This evaluation will illuminate an author's reasons for taking a particular stance on an issue and will aid in readers' evaluation of the author's ideas.

It is our hope that these books will give readers a deeper understanding of the issues debated and an appreciation of the complexity of even seemingly simple issues when good and honest people disagree. This awareness is particularly important in a democratic society such as ours in which people enter into public debate to determine the common good. Those with whom one disagrees should not be regarded as enemies but rather as people whose views deserve careful examination and may shed light on one's own.

Thomas Jefferson once said that "difference of opinion leads to inquiry, and inquiry to truth." Jefferson, a broadly educated man, argued that "if a nation expects to be ignorant and free . . . it expects what never was and never will be." As individuals and as a nation, it is imperative that we consider the opinions of others and examine them with skill and discernment. The Opposing Viewpoints Series is intended to help readers achieve this goal.

David L. Bender and Bruno Leone,
Founders

Introduction

> "A wage-price inflation spiral happens
> when wage rates feed back into goods
> and services prices. Wage earners
> demand, through political action—
> including through unions—wage
> increases indexed to inflation, increases
> in the minimum wage, and other
> policies that keep wages rising along
> with the prices of goods and services in
> the economy."
>
> —Eric Janszen, economics
> commentator and financial
> adviser

The minimum wage is the lowest hourly wage for work allowed by government. Inflation is the general rise in the prices of goods and services in an economy over time. The minimum wage and inflation may influence each other in a number of ways.

First, inflation may reduce the purchasing power of the minimum wage. The minimum wage is set by legislators. As inflation causes prices to rise, a worker making the minimum wage will be able to buy less and less. The push of inflation is often behind calls for a higher minimum wage. For example, a January 22, 2008, article by Jean Ross and Alissa Anderson Garcia in the *San Diego Union-Tribune* points out that, even with a recent boost in the minimum wage, California "only restore[d] low-wage workers' purchasing power to its 2002 level. The purchasing power of California's new minimum wage is still 24.8 percent below its 1968 purchasing power." Thus, although California had raised its minimum wage to eight dollars an hour, that wage could purchase relatively little compared with the minimum wage in 1968.

In order to stop inflation from eroding the minimum wage, Ross and Garcia suggest indexing the minimum wage to inflation. Rather than raising the minimum wage every so often when politicians decide to do so, Ross and Garcia say, the minimum wage should "automatically adjust each year to keep pace with the cost of living."

Some states have actually done this. Thus, while the un-indexed federal minimum wage drops in value every year, Washington state, for example, "automatically increases its minimum wage each year at the rate of inflation to make sure families don't face a *de facto* pay cut," states Caroline Fan in a January 8, 2009, article for the Progressive States Network. Other states beside Washington that index the minimum wage to inflation are Arizona, Colorado, Florida, Missouri, Montana, Nevada, Ohio, Oregon, and Vermont.

Some commentators have argued against indexing the minimum wage to inflation. A 2011 article on indexing the minimum wage on the website of the Economic Policy Institute (EPI) argues that indexing is futile since "a rising minimum wage has had no beneficial effect on reducing poverty." The same article argues that proponents of indexing systematically exaggerate the extent to which inflation erodes the minimum wage. Indexed minimum wages are usually pegged to the Consumer Price Index (CPI), a "crude tool that often overstates inflation," according to the EPI. Minimum wages pegged to the CPI rise too fast, according to the EPI. As a result, the EPI concludes, low-wage jobs are overpriced, which means employers will not hire people to fill those jobs, and so unemployment increases.

Other opponents of the minimum wage have argued that the minimum wage itself is responsible for increases in inflation. For example, a July 24, 2009, article in the *Wall Street Journal* argues that "raising the minimum wage is by definition inflationary. It adds to the cost of most anything with a basic labor component;

the price of thousands of consumer goods made in the US, the price of eating out at a low-priced restaurant, and the prices at most every struggling US retailer that counts on low-wage earners to turn the lights on and run the checkout stands." Businesses then pass the higher costs on to consumers in the form of higher prices. This drives up inflation.

Matthew B. Kibbe, in a May 23, 1988, policy analysis at the Cato Institute argues, however, that the minimum wage does not cause inflation to rise. He points out that if businesses experience increased costs, they are not always able to pass these on to consumers. "If a business cannot simply pass along its new labor costs, it must somehow absorb them—by eliminating workers rendered unproductive by the new minimum wage, by replacing labor with more-productive machines, or by cutting back production. Those jobs not eliminated will be more demanding, as employers will use fewer people to produce the same amount of work," Kibbe notes. In other words, increasing the minimum wage will not create inflation; instead, it will cause employers to eliminate jobs.

The viewpoints in this book address controversies surrounding the minimum wage in chapters titled What Impact Does the Minimum Wage Have on Workers? What Impact Does the Minimum Wage Have on Business and the Economy? How Does the Minimum Wage Affect Immigration? and What Are the Issues Surrounding the Minimum Wage in Other Countries? Authors of these viewpoints argue about whether the minimum wage should be raised, lowered, left alone, or eliminated altogether and what the policy effects of these changes would be.

CHAPTER 1

What Impact Does the Minimum Wage Have on Workers?

Chapter Preface

An internship is a system of on-the-job training for white-collar jobs. Many interns are paid less than minimum wage, and some even work for free. There has been some controversy about whether failing to pay interns minimum wage is exploitative.

According to the federal government's "Wage and Hour Divisions Fact Sheet #71" of April 2010, there are six criteria that must be applied to determine whether an intern may be unpaid. The criteria are:

- The internship, even though it includes actual operation of the facilities of the employer, is similar to training which would be given in an educational environment.
- The internship experience is for the benefit of the intern.
- The intern does not displace regular employees but works under close supervision of existing staff.
- The employer that provides the training derives no immediate advantage from the activities of the intern, and on occasion its operations may actually be impeded [by providing the internship].
- The intern is not necessarily entitled to a job at the conclusion of the internship.
- The employer and the intern understand that the intern is not entitled to wages for the time spent in the internship.

Steven Greenhouse, writing in an April 2, 2010, *New York Times* article, notes that many unpaid internships fail to meet these criteria. Greenhouse also reports that "the number of unpaid internships is mushrooming—fueled by employers' desire to hold down costs and students' eagerness to gain experience for their résumés." He concludes that while violations of federal guidelines are rampant, enforcing a fair wage for interns is difficult since the interns themselves are afraid to report violations for fear that they would be branded as troublemakers and would be unable to work in their chosen fields.

Kenneth Anderson, writing on the *Volokh Conspiracy* blog, responded to the *New York Times* article on April 5, 2010, in a short blog post in which he questions whether it would be wise to insist on a minimum wage for interns. He said it would be "hard for [him] to fathom" that higher wages for interns would be a boon. Anderson's implication was that if employers were forced to pay interns a minimum wage, they would simply hire fewer—or no—interns.

In an April 21, 2011, article in the *Oberlin Review*, on the other hand, Monica Klein argues that many progressive organizations violate their own principles in employing unpaid interns. Klein reports working as an unpaid intern at the liberal *Huffington Post*, then working as a salesperson at American Apparel in the evenings to make ends meet. She was thus working thirteen-hour days. "After three summers and one winter term, I have worked approximately 830 hours of unpaid labor," Klein writes. She concludes, "Many liberal news organizations will continue to argue for increased government spending and higher wages, while they simultaneously refuse to pay a large portion of their own workers."

The following chapter examines other controversies around the question of the minimum wage and its effects on workers.

> "The minimum wage has helped to maintain a basic standard of living for our lowest-income workers."

The Minimum Wage Helps Low-Income Workers

Kai Filion

Kai Filion is a policy analyst at the Economic Policy Institute. In the following viewpoint, he argues that the federal minimum wage helps the poorest people in society make ends meet and provide for their children. He also contends that the minimum wage helps to combat the recession by putting money in the hands of those who will spend it quickly and that lowering the minimum wage would not substantially increase employment. Filion argues that the minimum wage today is not especially high by historical standards and concludes that Congress should raise it.

As you read, consider the following questions:

1. According to Filion, what was the comparative worth of the minimum wage in 2006, adjusting for inflation?
2. What percentage of the workforce earns at or near the federal minimum wage in the thirty-six states where that wage is set at the federal level, according to the author?

3. What group of workers are not covered by the full minimum wage, according to Filion?

On each July 24th for the past three years [2007 through 2009], the federal minimum wage increased by $0.70. The last step of this three-part increase brought the minimum wage to $7.25 in 2009. One year later, we can now look at the data and see how this has had an impact on the economy. We find that the federal minimum wage is helping more than 5 million workers make ends meet, and 2.4 million of these workers' children depend on their earnings. The benefits of these increases went to low-income workers, who are most likely to put the money back into the economy. Finally, these increases provided a large stimulus to the economy at a time when this was desperately needed.

Federal and State Minimum Wages

The federal minimum wage was first established in the Fair Labor Standards Act of 1938. Since then, Congress has periodically increased the minimum wage as prices in the overall economy increased. In 2006, before the most recent three-part increase, the federal minimum wage was $5.15, the same level it had been for the previous 10 years. Because Congress had ignored the minimum wage for such a long time, inflation eroded much of its purchasing power. Adjusting for inflation, the minimum wage in 2006 was worth less than at any other time in the previous 50 years. Congress finally acted in 2007 to help low-wage workers, and passed a three-step increase to the federal minimum wage. The first increase to $5.85 took place on July 24, 2007, the second increase to $6.55 on July 24, 2008, and the final increase to $7.25 on July 24, 2009. Although this final step restored some of the purchasing power of the minimum wage, it is still well below the peak of close to $9.00 reached in 1968.

Around 2006, some states began to set their minimum wages above the federal minimum because Congress had ignored it for so long. In places where there is a state and a federal minimum

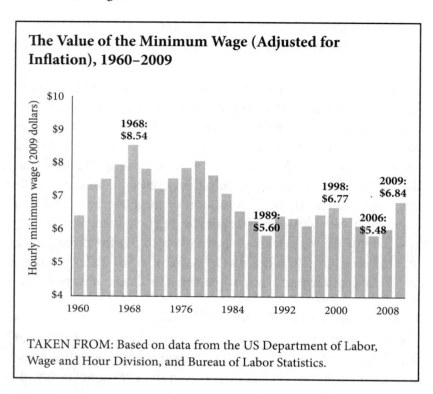

The Value of the Minimum Wage (Adjusted for Inflation), 1960–2009

1968: $8.54

1998: $6.77

2009: $6.84

1989: $5.60

2006: $5.48

TAKEN FROM: Based on data from the US Department of Labor, Wage and Hour Division, and Bureau of Labor Statistics.

wage, the higher of the two applies. In 2000, only 10 states and the District of Columbia had a higher minimum wage than the federal minimum. By the end of 2007, this increased to 30 states and the District of Columbia. Because of this state level action, the first federal increase in 2007 had a smaller impact than the third one, as the federal minimum wage was "catching up" in these states. There were only 19 states that were affected by the first increase, while the third one had an impact in 31 states. Today, there are only 14 states and the District of Columbia with a minimum wage higher than the federal minimum, with the highest set at $8.55 in Washington state.

A Basic Standard of Living

In the 36 states where the minimum wage is set at the federal level of $7.25, there are 5.4 million workers who earn at or near the federal minimum wage—about 4.4% of the total workforce in these states. These minimum wage workers include a disproportionate share of historically disenfranchised groups. About 60% of these workers are female, compared to 49% of the overall workforce, and 37% are either African American or Hispanic, compared to 26% in the overall workforce. Almost half of minimum wage workers are in families that earn under $35,000 a year. And the vast majority of this group, about 87%, do not have a college degree. Finally, there are 2.4 million children who depend on the income of these minimum wage workers.

In this recession [of 2010], the minimum wage has helped to maintain a basic standard of living for our lowest-income workers. Furthermore, research shows that increases to the minimum wage help to stimulate spending in the economy. We estimate that the second and third minimum wage increases boosted consumer spending by a total of $8.6 billion, precisely when the economy needed it most.

Lately, opponents of the minimum wage have suggested that decreasing it would help to boost employment. This is a terrible idea for a variety of reasons. First, the minimum wage is not high by historical standards—today, the real value of the minimum wage is less than what it was from 1961 to 1981. Second, research on the disemployment effects of the minimum wage give mixed results—many indicate that a small change to the minimum wage would have no impact on employment. Furthermore, even if there is a disemployment effect, it is small and far outweighed by the fact that low-wage workers on average will see a net benefit from most minimum wage increases. Finally, one of the biggest problems during a recession is the decrease in consumer demand—when consumers cut back on spending, employers respond by cutting back on jobs. Reducing the wages of already low-wage workers will only make this problem worse, and will hurt those who are least well off.

Barely Supporting Their Families

Today, the federal minimum wage is doing a better job of providing workers with a basic standard of living than before the recent three-step increase. However, for many workers, this is not enough. In real terms, the minimum wage is still below the level it reached from 1961 to 1981. The annual income of a full-time minimum wage worker (about $15,000) is almost the same as the poverty threshold for a family of two—in other words, minimum wage workers are barely able to support their families. And because the minimum wage is not adjusted for inflation, its purchasing power is already starting to erode. Finally, a large group of workers aren't directly covered by the full minimum wage—tipped workers in many states can be paid as little as $2.13 an hour.

One year after the last federal minimum wage increase, we see that this policy is helping those who need it the most. But we can do more. As the economy begins to recover from this recession, there are a few policies that will help to ensure that this growth also benefits those with low-incomes. First, the minimum wage should be set at a level that brings workers out of poverty. Second, the minimum wage should be indexed to wages, so that as workers in the overall economy gain, so do those who earn the least. And finally, the minimum wage for tipped workers should be increased so that these workers can count on a steady paycheck and their incomes are less vulnerable to the whims of customers.

| "*Higher minimum wages come at the cost of higher unemployment for low-skilled workers.*"

Minimum Wage Hikes Hurt Low-Income Workers

James Sherk

James Sherk is Bradley Fellow in Labor Policy at the Heritage Foundation. In the following viewpoint he argues that increases in the minimum wage cause employers to cut jobs for low-income and low-skilled workers. He says that during a recession these cuts for low-skilled workers will be particularly drastic and particularly painful. Not only will it deprive some workers of income, he argues, but it will prevent many workers from learning the job skills needed to get better jobs and wage increases. Sherk concludes that raising the minimum wage in a recession would damage both low-income workers and the economy.

As you read, consider the following questions:

1. By how much and in what increments did Congress raise the minimum wage starting in 2007, according to Sherk?
2. What does the author say is the true minimum wage?
3. According to Sherk, how much has the unemploy-

ment rate for teenagers risen since the beginning of the recession?

On July 24, [2009] the minimum wage increase Congress passed two years ago will enter its final phase, increasing the cost of hiring unskilled workers by 10 percent. Economic research demonstrates that higher minimum wages come at the cost of higher unemployment for low-skilled workers, but when Congress passed the minimum wage increase unemployment was low. Now, in the middle of a deep recession, unemployment has risen sharply for the least skilled workers. Wage growth has flattened since the start of the year [2009]. This minimum wage increase will artificially increase costs for struggling businesses at exactly the wrong time. And as a result, it will cost 300,000 teenagers and young adults their jobs.

The Wrong Time

Even advocates of a higher minimum wage should recognize that a recession is the wrong time to enact such legislation. Congress should postpone this minimum wage increase until the unemployment rates of teenagers and unskilled adults return to historically normal rates.

In 2007, Congress voted to increase the minimum wage, raising it in three $0.70 increments from $5.15 to $7.25 an hour. The first increase took place in July 2007, the second in July 2008, and the final increase will take effect on July 24, 2009. This final installment represents a 10 percent increase in the cost of hiring minimum wage employees.

The economy seemed healthy at the time that Congress passed the increase. Unemployment was below 5 percent. Since then the economy has slipped into a deep recession and unemployment has doubled to nearly 10 percent. Unemployment among the least skilled workers has jumped by an even larger amount. Congress should reconsider this minimum wage increase in light of the recession.

Congress trades off higher minimum wages against increased unemployment in all economic conditions because the true minimum wage is zero. Businesses will not hire workers whose labor produces less than the cost of hiring them. Employers will not pay $7.25 an hour to hire a worker whose hourly efforts bring in only an additional $7.00. Consequently, higher minimum wages price some less-skilled workers out of work. While some workers will get a raise, others will lose their jobs.

Most minimum wage research confirms this effect: Two-thirds of recent minimum wage studies find that it reduces employment, with the overwhelming majority of the most rigorous studies reaching this conclusion.

Although individual studies give different estimates, the typical results from research suggest that a 10 percent increase in the minimum wage will reduce employment among heavily affected groups of workers by roughly 2 percent. One study found that each 10 percent increase would cost 1.2 percent to 1.7 percent of low-income workers their jobs. Another study found that in the long term, a 10 percent increase in the minimum wage reduces teenage employment by 2.7 percent.

These estimates show that—under normal economic circumstances—this scheduled increase will cost 300,000 teenagers and young adults their jobs.

The Current Fiscal Climate

The current fiscal climate however, does not constituent "normal" economic circumstances. The economy is in a sharp recession, and most employers do not have the profits to pay higher wages. Nor can they pass costs on to consumers by raising prices, because Americans have become particularly budget conscious. Average wages did not grow in the last quarter.

The minimum wage increase amounts to an artificial 10 percent increase in the cost of hiring unskilled workers. Businesses always respond to higher costs by economizing, but they are especially sensitive to higher costs now. They will respond to this

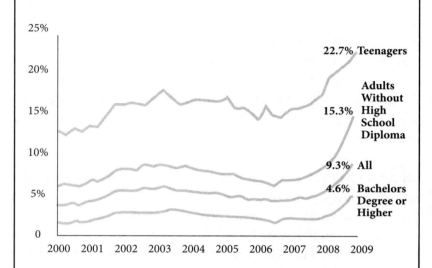

Unemployment Rate for Various Groups, 2000–2009

Teenagers are 16–19 years old and high school dropouts are 25 years of age or older.

22.7% Teenagers

Adults Without 15.3% High School Diploma

9.3% All

4.6% Bachelors Degree or Higher

TAKEN FROM: James Sherk, "Postpone Minimum Wage Increase Until Low-Skilled Unemployment Falls," Heritage Foundation, July 23, 2009. www.heritage.org. Data from: Department of Labor, Bureau of Labor Statistics/Haver Analytics.

minimum wage hike by trying to reduce their overall payroll costs as much as possible. They will reduce hours and cut even more jobs than would be expected in normal economic times. Wage growth has flattened since the start of the year because employers cannot afford to pay more.

The government should not discourage businesses from hiring unskilled workers right now. Whatever the debate over raising the minimum wage in normal times, unskilled workers cannot afford another 300,000 job losses now. . . . Unemployment has increased much more rapidly for less skilled workers than for Americans as a whole.

The overall unemployment rate has risen 4.5 percentage points since the start of the recession [in about 2008]. However, the unemployment rate for workers most affected by the minimum wage—teenagers and less educated adults—has risen at a much faster rate. Unemployment among teenagers has risen 6.4 percentage points to 22.7 percent. The unemployment rate for adults without a high school diploma has risen 7.8 percentage points to 15.3 percent. However, the unemployment rate for workers with a bachelor's degree or higher—almost none of whom earn the minimum wage—has only risen by 2.5 percentage points. Less-skilled workers have borne the brunt of job losses in the recession. Now is the wrong time to put another 300,000 employees out of work.

Putting 300,000 employees out of work would be particularly painful because minimum wage jobs provide unskilled workers with the opportunity to gain experience and become more productive. Few workers start at the minimum wage and stay there for decades. Rather, most minimum-wage jobs are entry-level positions and are typically taken by low-skilled workers with little workforce experience. Fully 40 percent of minimum-wage workers did not have a job in the previous year.

Minimum-wage jobs teach these workers valuable job skills, such as how to interact with customers and co-workers or accept direction from a boss—expertise that is difficult to learn without actual on-the-job experience. Once workers have gained these skills, they become more productive and earn higher wages. Two-thirds of minimum wage workers earn a raise within a year. Minimum-wage jobs provide valuable work experience that leads to higher-paying jobs—or that, during a recession, are needed to find employment. The minimum wage increase will saw off the bottom rung of the career ladder for many unskilled workers.

Already facing weak demand and flattening wage growth, businesses cannot afford an artificial 10 percent increase in their labor costs. Even supporters of raising the minimum wage should recognize that the government should not stimulate job losses in the middle of a recession. Congress should postpone the minimum wage increase until unemployment among the most affected workers returns to normal levels.

> *"In California, minimum wage is a ticket to enjoying more disposable income than the median wage earning family [has]."*

The California Minimum Wage Unfairly Enriches Low-Income Workers

Wayne Lusvardi

Wayne Lusvardi is a California journalist; he blogs at Pasadena Sub Rosa. *In the following viewpoint he argues that the minimum wage in California allows a worker to qualify for a number of welfare aid programs. He says that when you add in the benefits from these programs, a minimum-wage worker is actually able to make more than a median-income family. He concludes that this is unfair to median-income workers.*

As you read, consider the following questions:

1. How much more expendable income does a working family of four with one wage earner earning minimum wage have than the same family earning a median income, according to Lusvardi?

2. According to the author, what would have happened if state workers in California had been paid only minimum wage to cut the budget, as suggested by Governor Arnold Schwarzenegger?

3. What luxuries does Lusvardi say one can afford on a minimum wage?

Contrary to half-truths by both liberals who believe the minimum wage is a poverty wage or conservatives who believe it creates more unemployment and sends jobs overseas, at least in California, minimum wage is a ticket to enjoying more disposable income than the median wage earning family [has]—not through the mandated boost in wages, but because the minimum wage opens the door to myriad welfare programs paid for by tax dollars. Minimum wage is a ticket to qualifying for a number of aid programs that boosts a family's expendable income to almost 25 percent more than a California family earning the median income who do not qualify for any income assistance or tax credits.

Minimum Wage and Welfare

A working family of four with one wage earner at $8 per hour [the minimum wage] in California has 23 percent more expendable income, after receiving an earned income tax credit, food stamps, free school lunches, Medicaid and Section 8 housing assistance, than the same family earning the median income of $61,154 ($28 per hour) where an employer pays for the majority of medical insurance costs.

The stimulus for this conclusion is a Web post floating around the Internet claiming that a working family has more disposable income from a minimum wage job plus all the qualifying entitlements than if the same family was making the median income.

This writer tried to replicate this finding to see if it was valid but with more refined and documented data from California. A comparison was made in California of a family of four with one working parent and two school age children living in a two-bedroom apartment based on varying income levels and assumptions:

1. Part Time Worker—Working one week per month at minimum wage ($8/hour) assuming qualifying for free childcare, earned income tax credit, food stamps, school lunches, and Section 8 rental housing assistance.

2. Minimum Wage Worker—Working full time at minimum wage ($8/hour) assuming qualifying for free child care, earned income tax credit, food stamps, school lunches, and Section 8 rental housing assistance.

3. 50 percent Median Income Earner—Earning 50 percent of the median household income ($14/hour) assuming an employer pays the majority of medical insurance costs and household qualifies for earned income tax credit.

4.   Median Income Wage Earner—Earning the median household income ($28/hour) assuming an employer pays the majority of medical insurance costs.

It was assumed that all four families lived in a two-bedroom apartment in San Diego County where the county median household income ($62,820) is approximately the same as the state median income ($61,154). Rents, utility costs, transportation costs and household expenses were based on San Diego County data from the county housing authority and from the California Budget Project—2010: How Much Does It Cost To Raise a Family in California? The table summarizes the results of this exploratory study.

Minimum wage can't be looked at in isolation from the full cafeteria of income assistance programs for which it serves as an entry pass. Singularly looking at minimum wage is like finding the tree and missing the forest.

Minimum Wage Buys Votes

When Gov. Arnold Schwarzenegger called for state employees to be paid the minimum wage in lieu of their salaries to cure

California Minimum Wage Earners Compared to Median Household Earners

	Min. Wage	Medium Income
Money earned in a year	$16,000 @$8/hour	$61,154
Percent of Median Income	26%	100%
Payroll & Federal Income Taxes	($0)	($3,531)
Child Care Cost 2-School Age Children	$0	($10,792) 17.5%
California Income Tax	2% $0	9.3% ($1,366)
Earned Income Tax Credit	$5,036	0
Food Stamps CalFRESH	$8,016	0
School Lunch Program (NSLP)	$2,371	0
Medicaid CHIP	$0	($2,856)
Rent Cost with Section 8 Rent Subsidy	($4,350)	($18,000)
Utility Bill Cost with Subsidy	($1,450)	($1,200)
Transportation	($1,296)	($3,564)
Misc. Expenses	($479)	($479)
Total Expendable Income	$23,848	$19,366
Percent of Expendable Income of Median Family	123%	100%

TAKEN FROM: Adapted from Wayne Lusvardi, "CA Freebies Enrich Low-Wage Workers," CalWatchDog, November 29, 2010. www .calwatchdog.com.

the state budget deficit he must have known this would have increased the welfare burden in California, albeit possibly shifting it onto the federal government. State employees and unions may not have realized that minimum wage guaranteed more disposable income than the median income wage earner, albeit without all the lucrative retirement benefits and Cadillac medical insurance coverage [that state employees typically receive].

Given the symbiotic relationship between minimum wage and the whole bureaucratic vending machine of income assistance programs, California's perpetual budget deficits may have been even larger if the number of minimum hourly wage workers in California had not fallen from over 300,000 in 1998 to about 75,000 in 2007.

It may have been no coincidence that the [federal government's 2009] Cash For Clunkers program offered a $4,500 tax rebate to trade in an old car, paradoxically allowing the middle class wage earner to catch up with the net income of the minimum wage household instead of the other way around.

It is partly true that "the true minimum wage is zero" as economist Tom Sowell once stated if by this he meant that a minimum wage job might create two outsourced jobs in a zero sum game. Minimum wage has many aspects and many layers of meaning to different people depending on their social location.

But recipients of minimum wage in California apparently receive a $4,500 annual annuity for a family of four with one wage earner and two children. A $4,500 annual payment compounded at 5 percent over 30 years reflects about $10,000 per year. It is no wonder that Democratic politicians and unions argue for the minimum wage so strongly, for it surely must buy votes for an effective net income premium of $4,500 per year.

Working the System

This also refutes the half-truth that you "can't support a family on a minimum wage." It is true you can't support a family on minimum wage *alone*, but if you know how to work the system you can realize more net income than white-collar workers with much more education and training. To the contrary, you can support a family on a minimum wage and you can afford luxuries like a new car and a flat screen TV. Contrary to socialist U.S. Sen. Bernie Sanders of Vermont the minimum wage together with its qualifying income supplement programs is most definitely not "a poverty wage."

Where minimum wage jobs are given to undocumented persons who may not be able to qualify for the whole range of income assistance programs this would run counter to apparent social policy to wrap a "safety net" around minimum wage jobs. The whole package of minimum wage income supplement programs seems to follow a social policy that no full-time working family shall be deprived of the means to at least appear to be in the middle class.

The above comparison intentionally does not take into consideration other welfare transfers such as a homeowner's mortgage interest deduction because it only compared families in rental housing. Neither was a comparison made with two wage earner families, which would have also been [like comparing] apples and oranges. The above conclusions are tentative and are subject to modification based on better data and analysis or assumptions.

A provisional conclusion is that minimum wage in California is an annual winning lottery ticket not only into the middle class but a big leap-frog over the working class one earner family.

> *"Until we restore a stronger minimum wage for tipped workers, these jobs will continue to be a major contributor to the lower pay that women workers receive."*

A Higher Minimum Wage for Tipped Workers Would Help Women Especially

Rajesh D. Nayak and Paul K. Sonn

Rajesh D. Nayak is a former staff attorney and Paul K. Sonn is the Legal Co-Director at the National Employment Law Project. In the following viewpoint they argue that the real value of the minimum wage for tipped workers has fallen precipitously in recent years. As a result, they say, workers who rely on tips are struggling and many are sliding into poverty. The authors note that since women make up the largest number of tipped workers, the decline in the minimum wage hurts them especially. They recommend an increase in the minimum wage for tipped workers.

As you read, consider the following questions:

1. When was the minimum wage first enacted, and who did it exclude, according to the authors?

2. How many states have a higher minimum wage for tipped workers than the federal rate, according to Nayak and Sonn?

3. How much greater is the poverty rater of tipped workers than that of the workforce as a whole, according to the authors?

Today tipped industries are major sources of jobs in our nation's low-wage service economy. But at a meager $2.13 per hour under federal law, the tipped worker minimum wage is outdated and leaves millions of America's workers near poverty.

Tipped Workers and Minimum Wage

Tipped workers make up a significant portion of our low-wage service workforce. They work as parking attendants and car wash workers, nail salon workers and barbers, baggage porters and bellhops. The largest numbers are employed in food service where workers such as waitresses, waiters, bussers, and food delivery workers rely on tips. According to the federal Bureau of Labor Statistics, restaurants alone employ nearly 2.9 million workers in jobs that are generally classified as tipped positions. Food service is projected to be the twelfth fastest growing industry nationwide between 2006 and 2016. Moreover, recent trends suggest that tipped workers are increasing as a percentage of the minimum wage workforce in some states.

When it was first enacted in 1938, the federal minimum wage law, the Fair Labor Standards Act, did not cover most service and retail workers, including tipped workers such as waitresses and waiters. For decades after that, industry lobbyists fought proposals to extend minimum wage protections to this workforce, which represented many of the lowest paid jobs in the nation's economy. By the 1960s, the American Hotel and Motel Association estimated that the continued exemption of their employers from the minimum wage was saving the industry approximately $1 million each day.

In 1966, Congress finally overcame this opposition and extended minimum wage protections to most service and retail workers. But in doing so, it established the special tipped worker minimum wage, also known as the "tip credit." . . .

The industry would have preferred that employers not be required to pay tipped workers any wage at all, arguing that their tips generally added up to at least the minimum wage. However, Congress recognized that tip income is erratic and can subject workers to wide swings in pay as it fluctuates. It therefore established the tipped worker minimum wage to guarantee a stable base income that employers must pay their workers at all times, regardless of how much tip income they receive.

As a first step, Congress established this tipped worker minimum wage as 50% of the full minimum wage. Later, Congress phased it up to 60% in 1980. Other states have gone further and require employers to pay tipped workers 100% of the minimum wage as a cash wage. . . . Congress and most of the states also require that if workers' tips are not enough to bring them up to the full minimum wage, their employer must make up the difference. However, because most tipped workers make a few dollars more than the minimum wage, as a practical matter that requirement is seldom triggered.

When it is set at a substantial level, the tipped worker minimum wage boosts pay for most tipped workers to several dollars above the full minimum wage. Its function is to provide tipped workers an economic cushion and bring their pay closer to a living wage—something our economy needs more of today.

Just $2.13

When it established the tipped worker minimum wage in 1966, Congress set it as a fixed percentage of the full minimum wage, thereby linking the two minimum wage rates. This meant that when the minimum wage increased throughout the 1960s, 70s, 80s, and early 90s, the tipped worker minimum wage did too, ensuring that tipped workers did not fall behind.

In 1996, however, restaurant industry lobbyists prevailed on Congress to freeze the tipped worker minimum wage when it raised the overall minimum wage. Breaking with its nearly thirty-year practice of raising the tipped worker minimum wage whenever the minimum wage went up, Congress instead "de-linked" the two—freezing the minimum wage for tipped workers at $2.13. Over the next decade, both the minimum wage and the minimum wage for tipped workers languished as lawmakers ignored them. And when the new Congress elected in 2006 finally got President George W. Bush to sign a modest minimum wage increase in 2007, it left the minimum wage for tipped workers unchanged at $2.13.

As a result, both the relative value and the real value of the tipped worker minimum wage have fallen precipitously over the past two decades. In relative terms, its value has dropped from 60% of the minimum wage in 1990 to just 29% in 2009. In real terms, tipped worker minimum wage would be $4.89 today had it kept up with inflation over the last 40 years. Instead, it remains just $2.13, and its real value is at an all-time low.

During the years that Congress has allowed the tipped worker minimum wage to fall, many states have stepped in to adopt or preserve stronger tipped worker protections under their state minimum wage laws. States are able to do this because federal law allows states to establish their own minimum wages, and employers operating in the state must comply with the higher of the two.

Thirty-two states and the District of Columbia have established tipped worker minimum wages that are higher than the $2.13 federal rate. This includes twenty-two states that, as of 2010, will guarantee tipped workers at least 60% of the full minimum wage—the historical federal minimum wage rate for tipped workers. Seven of those states have gone further to guarantee tipped workers 100% of the minimum wage—a best practice that provides tipped workers a maximum cushion against economic insecurity and helps bring their pay closer to a living wage.

But despite this wave of action, eighteen states still have not strengthened their tipped worker minimum wages. Ten of those states have minimum wages for tipped workers that are the same as the low federal rate. And the remaining eight states provide no protection at all for tipped workers. New Jersey and Virginia, for example, have no tipped worker minimum wage and so allow workers to be paid entirely in tips. Georgia exempts tipped workers from its minimum wage coverage altogether. Five other Southern states—Alabama, Louisiana, Mississippi, South Carolina, and Tennessee—have no state minimum wage laws at all. In these states, millions of workers in the nation's high-growth tipped industries are protected only by the federal tipped worker minimum wage—which has languished at $2.13 since 1991. . . .

Keeping Women Near Poverty

The falling minimum wage for tipped workers is driving down living standards for the millions of America's workers—the vast majority of them adult women—who today spend their careers in the fast-growing tipped industries of our nation's service economy. In large part because of the low minimum wage, today, tipped workers like waitresses and waiters have nearly triple the poverty rate of the workforce as a whole. Until we restore a stronger minimum wage for tipped workers, these jobs will continue to be a major contributor to the lower pay that women workers receive across our economy.

According to the U.S. Census Bureau's Current Population Survey, tipped workers are overwhelmingly women, many of whom are supporting families. Overall, women make up 62% of tipped workers and 72% of waitresses and waiters—one of the largest groups of tipped workers. As a result, the tipped worker minimum wage is a substantial but underappreciated factor in the unequal wages that women workers continue to receive across our economy.

Making matters worse, even among tipped workers, women earn less. Overall, they average $0.40 less per hour than their

US Tipped Workers Demographics

(2005–2007, in 2007 dollars)

Demographic		Median Wage	Percent of Workforce
Overall		*$8.23*	*100.0%*
Education	No diploma	$7.25	32.3%
	High school grad	$8.50	31.9%
	Some college	$9.05	28.9%
	Bachelor's or more	$12.01	7.0%
Age	16–18	$7.00	20.7%
	19–20	$7.97	12.2%
	21–24	$8.50	18.8%
	25–44	$9.26	33.9%
	45–64	$9.50	14.5%
Race	White	$8.23	60.7%
	Black	$8.00	10.9%
	Hispanic	$8.23	20.8%
	Other	$8.80	7.6%
Gender	Male	$8.50	38.1%
	Female	$8.10	62.0%

TAKEN FROM: Rajesh D. Nayek and Paul K. Sonn, "Restoring the Minimum Wage for America's Tipped Workers," National Employment Law Project, August 2009, p. 11. http://nelp.3cdn.net/ bff44d5fafbd9d2175_vem6ivjjb.pdf.

male counterparts. For restaurant workers the differential is even larger: waitresses average $0.70 per hour less than waiters.

Nor are tipped workers chiefly teenagers, as industry lobbyists often suggest. More than two-thirds of tipped workers are adults twenty-one and older, as are 72% of waitresses and waiters.

Industries employing tipped workers represent some of the lowest paid jobs in the U.S. economy. In fact, the U.S. Department of Labor's Bureau of Labor Statistics cites food preparation and service as the nation's single lowest paying industry. Other industries employing tipped workers, such as nail salons and car washes, also pay poverty-level wages.

Even after accounting for tips, the vast majority of tipped workers are still barely getting by. According to our analysis of Current Population Survey [CPS] data from 2005–2007, tipped workers nationwide earn a median wage of $8.23 per hour including tips, or just $17,118 annually (in 2007 dollars). Waitresses and waiters earn slightly more, but still only $9.00 per hour including tips or $18,720 annually—barely more than the poverty level for a family of three and less than the poverty level for a family of four. As a result, a sizeable percentage of waitresses and waiters live in families below the poverty level—and the rates are even higher for black and Hispanic waitresses and waiters.

Overall, the family poverty rate for waitresses and waiters is 14.9%—almost three times the rate for the workforce as a whole. And the rates are even higher for tipped workers as a whole, since their wages are lower than those of waitresses and waiters.

Moreover, it is widely recognized that the federal poverty level is artificially low and substantially underestimates the income that an individual or a family needs to avoid economic hardship in the United States. In reality, even a single adult cannot make ends meet on the $9.00 per hour that the average waitress earns. More realistic calculations show that breadwinners need to earn closer to $19.00 per hour, or $40,000 per year, to actually meet basic needs, depending on family size and the local cost of living.

Low Wages and High Poverty

It is true that there exists some economic diversity among tipped workers, who can work in a variety of different workplaces with varying levels of tips. But while some waitresses and waiters at high-end restaurants may earn high incomes, they represent a very small minority of restaurant workers, and an even smaller portion of tipped workers overall. Across the country, data suggest that only the top quarter of waitresses and waiters earned more than $12.86 per hour in wages and tips or $26,748 per year during 2003–2007. And the median wage was just $9.00. But even this number hides the fact that wages are lower for waitresses and waiters in most of the states, since it includes—and is therefore inflated by—wages in states like California, Oregon, and Washington that both have relatively high state minimum wages and require tipped workers to be paid 100% of the minimum wage. In the eighteen states where the tipped worker minimum wage is effectively stuck at $2.13, the median wage for waitresses and waiters was just $8.40.

Moreover, tipped workers must stretch their wages further because they are less likely than other workers to receive employer-provided health insurance. Waitresses and waiters are only one-quarter as likely as the workforce as a whole to have a health insurance plan under which their employer pays some portion of the cost. As a result, these workers are twice as likely to go without health insurance.

The data on waitresses and waiters—the largest group of tipped workers—are the most readily available for illustrating these problems. But other tipped workers earn even less. For example, the median hourly wage for all tipped workers for whom data were available (excluding waitresses and waiters, bartenders, and food preparation workers) was just $8.16 per hour during 2005–2007. This group includes hotel and restaurant workers not involved in food preparation, barber shop workers, and other personal services workers to name a few.

Interviews with tipped workers illustrate how many struggle to make ends meet. One restaurant worker living in an apartment complex near Philadelphia explained that in order to afford the car that she needs to get to her job, she must share a one-bedroom apartment with two other restaurant workers. Her monthly expenses consume all of her income, leaving her unable to afford to take time off or improve her living arrangements. Another waitress living in New Jersey described how she struggles to raise her two young children on her meager earnings, and was forced to turn to a homeless shelter until she received a temporary housing voucher that enabled her to afford an apartment. "When you wait tables," she explained, "you're not even check to check, but day to day."

But waitresses and waiters still make more than other tipped restaurant workers like bussers and runners. As a waiter named Juan Carlos remembered from his time bussing tables in a New Brunswick, New Jersey chain restaurant before becoming a waiter, "The money you make per hour, it's not worth it. I made $40, from 5PM to 12 [midnight]. . . . There are three guys, and you have to break the tips in three. And the morning is the worst. You start working at 10:00 and end at 3:00 and the tips are really bad, I'm talking $20." As a result, his living situation was fairly typical: "We were five guys sharing one room. It's not a very good experience."

"Growing inequality in the labor market . . . and stagnant federal minimum-wage laws have increased the oxymoron of full-time, year-round working poor people."

A Low Minimum Wage Hurts Women, Children, and Minorities

William E. Spriggs

William E. Spriggs chairs the department of economics at Howard University. He is a senior fellow at the Economic Policy Institute and former executive director of the National Urban League Institute for Opportunity and Equality. In the following viewpoint, Spriggs outlines how public policy can influence poverty. Legislation, such as minimum wage laws, has not done enough to protect the poor, who are largely, (and disproportionately) women, children, and minorities. Spriggs discusses the correlation of race with state policies to address poverty, as well as intractable issues that have made the face of poverty primarily young, black, Hispanic, and female.

As you read, consider the following questions:

1. According to the author, what must one do to "put a face on American poverty"?

William E. Spriggs, "The Changing Face of Poverty in America," Ending Poverty in America, a special report of *The American Prospect*, vol. 18, no. 5, May 2007. Copyright © 2007 The American Prospect, Inc. Reproduced by permission.

2. During what era, according to the author, did "poverty win"?
3. Among the poor, what percent work full-time, year round?

Water, water everywhere, nor any drop
to drink.

—*Samuel Taylor Coleridge,*
The Rime of the Ancient Mariner

I n 1960 American workers produced a Gross Domestic Product [GDP] of $13,847 (in year 2000 dollars) for every man, woman, and child in the country. By 1969, GDP per capita rose to $18,578. In that period, the poverty rate for American children dropped almost by half, from 26.5 percent to 13.8 percent. The most recent data, for 2005, show child poverty has risen again, to 17.1 percent, while the GDP per capita stood at $37,246, roughly double the value in 1969. How did the nation become twice as wealthy but its children become poorer?

In 2000, the number of poor Americans reached an 11-year low at 31.6 million, and the poverty rate stood at a 26-year low at 11.3 percent. While the nation again became richer after the post-2001 recovery, more than 5 million Americans fell into poverty, and the latest figures put the number of poor Americans at 36.9 million people.

To put a face on American poverty, it is important to first put that poverty in context—to understand not just who is poor today but to examine how poverty changes over time. With that perspective, we can appreciate that in a nation as wealthy as the United States, poverty is not intractable.

The federal government declared war on poverty, and poverty won.

—*Ronald Reagan*

That line from President Reagan's 1988 State of the Union address was used to ridicule Lyndon Johnson's efforts to fight poverty. President Johnson launched that fight in March 1964, submitting the Economic Opportunity Act to Congress and saying these words: "Because it is right, because it is wise, and because, for the first time in our history, it is possible to conquer poverty. . . ".

Johnson believed that a wealthy nation produces enough for each individual citizen to live above poverty. This was a question of political and moral will, not an economic constraint. So, he differentiated between the day's global struggle to end poverty in countries like Mali and Haiti, where there was a real economic constraint to be overcome, and the situation in America, a land that was not poor in resources but that lacked moral conviction. . . . In 1965, almost 66 percent of black children lived below the poverty line. In four short years, that share was cut to 39.6 percent, a tremendous accomplishment. By contrast . . . poverty for black children [rose] from 1981 to 1989, the era of Reagan and George Bush Senior. In 1980, 42.1 percent of black children lived below the poverty line; and by 1988 that share had risen to 42.8 percent. Yes, poverty won.

How Policy Influences Poverty

The face of poverty in America is the result of policy choices, of political will, and of moral conviction—or its absence. The incidence of poverty is heavily concentrated in the United States across the South and the Southwest. The legacy of slavery is part of that story. Forty percent of America's poor live in the South. Four of today's five poorest states were ones that existed in the old Confederacy. Of the onetime Confederate states, only two—Florida and Virginia—do not rank in the current 20 states with highest poverty levels.

Why do some people lack the income to rise above poverty? For many, the reason is that they do not work; for others, the reason is that they work but do not earn enough money. Nonworkers include the elderly, the disabled, and children, as well as the unemployed. And public policy treats different groups differently.

The Social Security old-age program insures virtually all retired workers against the risk of outliving their savings. The old-age benefit formula is tied to the rising productivity of current workers, indexing the benefits to the average national wage. The shared risk, and the insured shared prosperity, explain why the poverty rate for those over 65 has declined from more than 28 percent in 1966 (nearly double the national poverty rate of 14.7 percent) to 10.1 percent today (below the national rate of 12.6 percent). In 1974, the poverty rate for the Census category of white non-Hispanic seniors, at 12.5 percent, was double the poverty rate for working-age (18-64) white non-Hispanics, at 5.9 percent. Today, the poverty rate for the two age groups is virtually equal, at 7.9 percent for seniors and 7.8 percent for working-age white non-Hispanics.

Another group of people who do not work, by law, are children. But their income is derived mostly from their parents. The rise in child poverty, therefore, reflects the rise in the inequality of their parents' earnings. So, while 9.8 percent of the poor are seniors, 33.5 percent of the poor are children. Children make up a much higher share of the poor among blacks (41.9 percent of poor blacks) and Hispanics (42.6 percent of poor Hispanics) than among whites (24.5 percent of poor whites). And while the poverty rate of seniors has shown a steady trend downward as national income has risen, child poverty rates are as intractable as the growing inequality in working families' earnings.

The wide divergence in how public policy treats different groups was not Congress' original intent. The Social Security Act of 1935 sought to protect the incomes of those who did not work because of age or a poor economy by establishing a federal framework for unemployment insurance, old-age benefits, and assistance to women with dependent children. In 1939, the old-age benefit structure was fully federalized to produce consistent benefits. But Aid to Families with Dependent Children (AFDC) and the unemployment-insurance system were put in state hands. And in the 1990s, AFDC was transformed from its Social Security Act roots into a state block grant. The mostly state-run unemployment-insurance system, meanwhile, is strained by the transformation of the economy from one in which workers could expect to be laid off in recessions and then rehired into one based on the structural creation and destruction of whole industries and occupations.

Children in our antipoverty system are oddly split. Today, more children receive a check from the Old Age, Survivors and Disability Insurance (OASDI) Program than are helped by the new Temporary Assistance for Needy Families (TANF) program that replaced AFDC. Some children, therefore, enjoy their parents' protection against the loss of income from disability, untimely death, or old age, and receive benefits that are based on the same formula used for the old-age benefit. Low-income black children are especially helped by the disability benefits their parents receive, or by the survivor benefits that the child receives—because the benefit formula is national and intended to alleviate poverty.

By contrast, children receiving TANF aid are subject to the whim of their state. In 2004, a widowed mother and two children, on average, received a monthly OASDI survivors' benefit of $1,952. Those two children would live above the federal poverty line. The TANF benefit for the same family, however, could range from $170 a month in Mississippi to $215 in Alabama to $240 in Louisiana to $625 in New Hampshire, leaving children in all of those states far below the poverty line. Adjusting for inflation, the survivors' benefit has been increasing since 1970, while the average benefit under AFDC (and now TANF) has been falling. While the OASDI benefit level is set by a federal formula, policy-makers in states with higher shares of black TANF recipients choose lower benefit levels.

Like TANF recipients, unemployed workers are also at the mercy of their state; the average weekly benefit can range from

$179 a week in Mississippi to $320 in New Jersey. In the 1950s, close to half of the nation's unemployed workers received benefits; today, only about 35 percent do. This varies widely by state, from 21 percent in Wyoming to 24 percent in Texas to 58 percent in Pennsylvania to 71 percent in New Jersey. And the percentage of earned income replaced by unemployment benefits has steadily fallen as well.

Diligent and Still Poor

An ongoing topic of debate is the relationship of child poverty and parents' income to the increase in single-parent households. Other things being equal, two parents in a household usually earn more than one, but they are not assured of earning their family's way out of poverty. Hispanic and black children have roughly similar levels of poverty—33.2 percent for black children, and 27.7 percent for Hispanic children. Yet 41 percent of black families with children are married, whereas 68 percent of Hispanic families with children are married. In 1974, when the poverty rate among black children was at 39.6 percent, 56 percent of black families with children were married. Two-income families today are less likely to be poor, but much is at work besides family structure.

To be poor is to lack income, so the core issue is earnings. In 1962, on the eve of the March on Washington for Jobs and Justice in 1963, the median income of black men was below the poverty threshold for a family of three, but by 1967 it was above that level (not until 1995 did it get above the poverty level for a family of four). Because of the rise in the earnings of black women, poverty among black children fell in the 1990s, just as the rise in the earnings of black men helped lower black children's poverty level in the 1960s. By 1997, the median income of black women rose above the poverty level for a family of three.

Among the poor, 11.4 percent work full time, year-round. These 2.9 million Americans are directly hurt by minimum-wage laws that have lagged behind costs of living. This problem is especially acute for Asians and Hispanics, where 18 percent of the working poor worked full time, year-round.

Recent immigrants who are not citizens have a poverty rate of 20.4 percent. Like all groups, noncitizen immigrants had falling poverty rates in the 1990s as the labor market expanded: Their poverty rate fell from 28.7 percent in 1993 to a low of 19.2 percent in 2000. Then, following the national trend, their poverty rate started to climb. During the Reagan administration, the United States suffered its highest national unemployment rates since the Great Depression. In the black community, the effects were devastating: The unemployment rate for adult (over age 20) black men peaked at more than 20 percent in December 1982; during the entire Reagan presidency, the unemployment rate for adult black men remained in double digits. The highest recorded unemployment rate for adult white men was 9 percent in November and December 1982. But for black men, the unemployment rate remained above that mark for 182 straight months (15 years), from October 1979 to November 1994. Because children do not work and need working adults to support them, it is hardly surprising that during that period, black child poverty rates remained intractable above 40 percent.

Poverty for women is disproportionately higher than for men, 14.1 percent compared to 11.1 (in 2005), primarily because of higher rates of poverty among female-headed households, gaps in poverty for the elderly (7.3 percent for men over age 65 compared to 12.3 percent for women in 2005), and for single women (24.1 percent) compared to single men (17.9 percent) living alone. The gap reflects persistent gaps in earnings between men and women, though that gap is falling. White non-Hispanic men, age 25 and over, with a high-school diploma have a median income of $35,679, while women, age 25 and over, need a college degree to have a similar median income ($36,532 in 2005). And, while the median income of white males has been above the poverty line for a family of five since 1959, the median income for women only broke above the poverty line for a family of three in

1990. The persistent gap is best reflected in differences in poverty among the elderly, where the life-long earnings of women mean they have lower assets in Social Security benefits than do men, despite the progressive structure of the benefit formula. The gap among the elderly also reflects issues of access to jobs with pensions for women.

Women who are the single heads of household face the extra burden of earning enough to raise dependent children out of poverty. This risk a woman faces of helping non-working dependents is not shared by society, as would be a woman's efforts to care for her elderly parents. The result is that female-headed households, harmed by the significant earnings gap between men and women, have a poverty rate of 31.1 percent compared to male-headed households (with no wife present) of 13.4 percent, while the overall poverty rate for families is 10.8 percent.

Full Employment and Its Limits

It took the presidency of Bill Clinton, with its expansive labor market and increases in the minimum wage and the Earned Income Tax Credit, to dramatically improve the incomes of poor and minority families. As job creation reached a record pace, the unemployment rate for black men plummeted, reaching a recorded low of 6 percent in March 1999. With work comes income, and poverty for black families fell. This history suggests something about the proper way to view responsibility and poor people as agents in their own fate: Usually they are not victims of themselves, but of bad economic policies and barriers to opportunity.

Under Reagan, who ridiculed antipoverty efforts, the number of black children living below the poverty line increased by 200,000, from 3.9 million in 1980 to 4.1 million in 1988. During the Clinton years, the black child poverty rate fell steadily, from 46.3 percent to a record-low 30 percent, lifting about 1.6 million black children out of poverty. For all children, the poverty rate fell annually during Clinton's presidency, reaching a 30-year low of 15.6 percent when he left office. But those reduced poverty rates may be the best we can achieve simply by getting jobs for parents. While lower than during the Reagan years, they do not equal the lows America has achieved for its senior citizens, or the general population. And those gains reversed course when George W. Bush became president.

Because of record job creation in the 1990s, the number of people who worked and were poor declined from 10.1 million in 1993 to 8.5 million by 2000; greatly increased working hours and higher wages meant higher incomes. But during the current expansion, a record 48 months was required to get payroll employment back to the level preceding the employment downturn that began in late 2000, a lag not matched since Herbert Hoover. So while full employment is necessary to alleviate poverty, it is far from sufficient.

In short, America knows how to address poverty. Its great success in lowering the poverty level of those over 65 has changed the face of poverty. But for those subject to the whims of state differences and the correlation of race with state policies to address poverty, there have been great intractable issues that have left the face of poverty disproportionately young, black, Hispanic, and female. Growing inequality in the labor market, moreover, has increased the share of the poor who are of working age, and stagnant federal minimum-wage laws have increased the oxymoron of full-time, year-round working poor people.

In a nation with a per capita GDP above the poverty line for a family of four, it is appalling that almost 3 million people work full time, year-round and are poor, and that more than 12 million American children are living in poverty. Lyndon Johnson proposed to fight poverty "because it is right, because it is wise." In a land of vast wealth, twice as rich as America in the 1960s, can today's leaders to rise to the occasion?

> *"The minimum wage hike has . . . forced employers to lay off . . . young people who had their first real job—causing an overall rise in black unemployment."*

The Minimum Wage Hurts Black Teen Workers

Richard W. Rahn and Izzy Santa

Richard W. Rahn is a senior fellow at the Cato Institute and chairman of the Institute for Global Economic Growth; Izzy Santa is an adjunct researcher at the Center for Freedom and Prosperity. In the following viewpoint, they argue that raising the minimum wage causes employers to lay off low-income workers. They say that this policy particularly hurts black teen workers. They argue that government programs to alleviate unemployment are less effective than simply eliminating the minimum wage would be.

As you read, consider the following questions:

1. In March 2010, when the viewpoint was written, what was the unemployment rate for black teenaged males, according to the authors?
2. Why do Rahn and Santa say that few people advocate for a federal minimum wage of $100/hr?

3. Under what conditions do the authors say employers will hire more workers?

Congress believes it has the solution to America's epidemic of joblessness: a so-called jobs bill whose centerpiece is a tax credit for companies that hire one of the 15 million unemployed.

Rising Unemployment

Many legislators from the Congressional Black Caucus criticize the bill for not going far enough. And they are right. It doesn't remove one of the many factors that has caused higher unemployment: a government-imposed minimum wage.

Today [March 2010], black unemployment is almost 16 percent and was at a 25-year high, even as the overall unemployment rate declined from 10 percent to 9.7 percent.

Teenaged black males, whose unemployment rate is currently 44.9 percent, up from 39.2 in July [2009] (when the minimum wage hike took effect), have been hurt the most by the recession. In fact, November—five months after the wage hike—saw unemployment for this demographic reach 57.1 percent—the second highest rate on record at the Bureau of Labor Statistics.

Three years ago, then-Sen. [Barack] Obama and prominent African-American organizations thought a hike in the minimum wage would empower minorities.

So how much should workers be paid? $100 per hour? $25 per hour? $7.25 per hour (the current federal rate)? Or zero? For 95 percent of workers a wage of a $100 per hour would be a significant raise. But most people understand that very few people would have jobs at a minimum wage of $100 per hour—so there are few, if any, advocates for that rate.

After a nine-year battle, when July's increase in the minimum wage took effect, the Democratic Policy Council declared, "This was a long overdue raise for American workers." Maybe for some workers, but the 3 million blacks currently unemployed are now feeling the pain.

The minimum wage hike has cost employers more, an additional $2.10 per hour, and forced employers to lay off many minimum-wage workers—most of them young people who had their first real job—causing an overall rise in black unemployment.

Ignoring Basic Economics

Think back to when you were a teenager, and needed, or wanted some extra cash. Would you have been better off not getting a job at the set minimum wage, or would you have been better off getting a job at 20 percent less than the minimum wage at the time? It's hard to argue that no job is better than a lesser paying job.

These alarming unemployment figures have now prompted the Congressional Black Caucus and others who advocated for higher wages to fix their first mistake by asking the President and Congress to develop a job creation plan that targets areas of chronic unemployment.

Congress' latest jobs proposal, however, completely undermines the argument for a higher minimum wage. The logic for the tax credit is that if labor becomes cheaper, by way of a credit subsidy, businesses will hire more people. The cognitive dissonance on display is astounding.

Employers will hire more workers of any given experience and skill level when the cost of doing so is lower. The fact is, few people stay at the minimum wage for very long. Once they learn basic job skills—showing up on time, working hard, and the mechanics of the job they are doing—their value to their employers increases, which is reflected in higher wages.

It is unconscionable that these young people with relatively few skills are prevented from being productive members of society because politicians choose to ignore basic economics. The fastest and most straightforward way to empower minorities and reduce unemployment is to end the imposition of mandatory minimum wages at levels well above what the market can afford.

But, as is the case all too often in Washington, politics trumps rational argument and true compassion.

In 1968, weeks before his death, Martin Luther King Jr. said, "If a man doesn't have a job or an income, he has neither life nor liberty nor the possibility for the pursuit of happiness. He merely exists."

In this case, the ones merely existing are the most disadvantaged, in particular, black male teenagers who pay the price with their forcible exclusion from the work force.

| *"There are lots of reasons to take a minimum-wage job, but the lack of better-paying work almost certainly isn't one of them."*

Most Teens Can Find Jobs Paying More than Minimum Wage

Kevin D. Williamson

Kevin D. Williamson is a writer and editor. In the following view-point, he argues that most low-paying jobs pay more than mini-mum wage already. He also says that low-paying jobs are generally held by teens on their first jobs. He concludes that the argument over minimum wage is therefore not relevant for the vast majority of teen workers. He also argues that Americans should have more respect for those who work outside an office, whether for minimum wage or not.

As you read, consider the following questions:

1. According to Williamson, what are the wages for some low-paying jobs in the area where he lives?
2. How did Burger King illegally exploit the author, and why was he happy about them doing so?

3. What would Williamson prefer over arguments about the minimum wage?

O ne of the unlovely traditions of American politics is the annual Labor Day fight over minimum wage. Never mind that about one percent of U.S. workers earn the minimum wage. Like stem cells and school choice, the debate over minimum wage isn't really about what we all pretend it's about.

Making More than Minimum Wage

I've never made minimum wage. There is no need to do so. There are lots of reasons to take a minimum-wage job, but the lack of better-paying work almost certainly isn't one of them. I grew up poor and have held some humble jobs—Burger King fry-guy and 7-Eleven graveyard-shift polyester-smock-wearer among them—and I've never even been offered minimum wage. In my neighborhood in the D.C. suburbs, fast-food joints are offering upwards of $9 an hour plus free meals. Answering phones at the pet day-care center gets you $11/hour, making phone calls for a local survey company gets you $13/hour. Working as an assistant at an art gallery's web store gets you $40,000 a year plus benefits. Doggie day care and art galleries: Damn you, heartless capitalism!

In my earlier jobs I didn't make a lot more than minimum wage, true, and I certainly could have made a lot more money working as a roofer, warehouse hand, or tile-installer. I worked at Burger King because it was an easy job to get and because it was close enough to my house that I could walk to work—I wasn't old enough to drive, so that was a real consideration. I worked at 7-Eleven because I was going to stay up all night reading, anyway, and 7-Eleven paid me to do so. It doesn't take that long to clean the Slurpee machine and straighten up the frozen burritos every night, and Lubbock, Tex., where I grew up, isn't exactly bustling with business at 4 A.M. on a Tuesday.

The Value of Being Exploited

Working at Burger King actually turned out to be a pretty good gig. (I've had worse jobs—much worse—many of which paid much more.) I was a vegetarian at the time, so I spent the summer living on Burger King salads and lost about 30 pounds. But the great thing was that they illegally exploited me. The local Burger King franchise-owner decided to complement a dozen of his establishments with those "playscapes" designed to entice little kids into pestering their parents to take them to Burger King. They needed somebody to help build playscapes, but didn't want to go through the hassle of hiring a crew to do the work. So they paid me $10 an hour on top of my not-minimum wage to assemble giant nets full of rubber balls and plastic slides. They also gave me coupons for about 100 free Whoppers, which I distributed to my carnivorous friends. Of course I was paid in cash, without benefits or Social Security contributions, and of course I was working more hours than a 15-year-old is supposed to be allowed to work. But I was happy to be making $15 an hour back when minimum wage was something like $3.15. I didn't feel exploited. I wanted more hours.

I worked the late-night shift at Burger King, and we stayed open late enough to catch the drunker-than-Cooter-Brown/high-as-a-Georgia-pine after-hours trade from the honky-tonk across the street. Our dining room was full of hungry, boot-scootin' drunks at 3 A.M.—one of them blazed enough to ask me "What do you recommend?" as though I were maître d' at the Four Seasons. But I had the good fortune to work with a really good fast-food crew managed by a former West Point cadet named Wally. As a West Point fish Wally had been assigned the "job" of being a human doorknocker for an upperclassman and was obliged to spend several hours each evening hanging from said upperclassman's door. Not appreciating how this was going to prepare him to help defend our republic against all foes, foreign and domestic, Wally quit West Point and worked as a Burger King assistant manager to put himself through college. He ran a good burger joint—good enough that people left us tips, which is fairly unusual for a fast-food gig. Wally—now Prof. Wally to you, MBA, Ph.D—is happily ensconced in a good university chair these days.

Burger King kept me occupied all summer, fed me free salads and endless Diet Pepsis, and, best of all, paid me well enough that I still had a little money left over after buying some back-to-school gear and a beautiful old Gibson guitar of the sort made famous by Chuck Berry. Most people who earn minimum wage aren't heads of households. They're young people in their first jobs, saving up for guitars, used cars, or Spring Break ski trips. In our nation of 300 million souls, about 500,000 people earn the minimum wage, according to the Labor Department. In fact, there are about three times that many people being paid illegally low wages, the government estimates. Even so, more than 90 percent of our 12 million illegal immigrants are making better than minimum wage. Remember those raids on the meatpacking plant in Greeley, Colo.? Those illegals were making about $10 an hour—as a starting wage. Those who'd been there for a while were earning more, of course.

I've done all sorts of things for money—I've been a bouncer-for-hire at frat parties, a writing tutor, a lawn mower, and a newspaper editor—at one point, an illegal immigrant newspaper editor in India. I once had a job shoveling ice into a hole for the Coca-Cola Bottling Co., which paid me more than twice minimum wage for doing a job that could have been performed by a reasonably well-trained monkey. When I was an unemployed newspaper editor, I wrote copy for furniture catalogs. *Philadelphia Bulletin* reporter Jim McCaffrey and I once even made extra cash by pretending to be tough guys on behalf of a rent-collector in New Jersey. And McCaffrey's a professional Tarot card reader, among other things. Opportunity abounds.

Working Outside an Office

I'm not going to offer a Labor Day hymn to the value of honest hard work, because I'd honestly hardly work at all if I didn't have an appetite for things that cost money. But I do resent like hell people who quietly disdain working-class Americans and the jobs they do, as though to work outside of an office is to have somehow failed at life.

I have an acquaintance who runs an auto-body shop, and I've heard it said of him that he is so smart that he should have gone to college and "made something of himself." That's hogwash. Setting aside the fact that as the owner of an auto-body shop this fellow earns about twice what your typical lawyer manages to shanghai from honest folks in a year, he's running his family business, started making decent money while he was still in high school, got married and had a bunch of kids while he and his wife were still young enough to enjoy them, takes care of his own, and makes his town a better place. He did make something out of himself, and his house was paid for before he was 30. I envy the guy: His wife and kids actually seem to like him, and he has a 1964 Impala done up so sweet it could give you cavities. So maybe he never read Marcus Aurelius [a Roman emperor known for his philosophical writings]. You know what? Most college graduates never read Marcus Aurelius, either. They take Literature Lite and get degrees that enable them to spend their days watching spreadsheets and their nights watching working-class people laboring on *Pimp My Ride* [a television reality show about restoring cars]. You think the guys who live *Pimp My Ride* go home and watch somebody edit spreadsheets at night?

Rather than spending every Labor Day bickering about the minimum wage, I'd like to see the Powers That Be make it easier for creative 15-year-olds to start learning to become welders, metal fabricators, or carpenters. It would be a far better thing than treating them like they're lazy or retarded because they don't have much interest in poetry or algebra.

Periodical and Internet Sources Bibliography

The following articles have been selected to supplement the diverse views presented in this chapter.

Simon Akam	"Tipped Workers Left Out as Minimum Wage Rises," *New York Times*, July 23, 2009.
Bruce Bartlett	"Minimum Wage Teen-Age Job Killer," NCPA, May 20, 1999. www .ncpa.org.
Angry Bear	"Teen Unemployment and the Minimum Wage," March 15, 2010. www.angrybearblog.com.
Nancy Folbre	"Along the Minimum-Wage Battle Front," *New York Times* blog, November 1, 2010. http://econo mix.blogs.nytimes.com.
Craig Garthwaite	"High Minimum Wage = High Unemployment," *Seattle Post-Intelligencer*, December 26, 2003.
Tsedeye Gebreselassie and Paul Sonn	"Women and the Minimum Wage," *American Prospect*, July 24, 2009.
Lia Mandaglio	"Minimum Wage Reform Will Give Millions of Black Workers a Pay Raise," The Leadership Conference, March 12, 2007. www .civilrights.org.
Ruth Mantell	"Women and the Federal Minimum Wage," *Wall Street Journal*, September 11, 2008.
Seeking Alpha	"Teen Employment: The Impact of Minimum Wage Hikes," March 11, 2011. http://seekingalpha.com.
Paul Sonn and Rajesh D. Nayak	"Tipped Workers and the Minimum Wage," *Huffington Post*, July 22, 2009.
Clifford F. Thies	"The First Minimum Wage Laws," *Cato Journal*, Winter 1991.
Walter Williams	"Collusion Against Our Youth," *New American*, December 16, 2009.

CHAPTER 2

What Impact Does the Minimum Wage Have on Business and the Economy?

Chapter Preface

Economists and commentators have debated the relationship between the minimum wage and high school drop-out rates for a long time. The relationship is important in part because high school dropouts earn lower wages long term, affecting their own quality of life and placing a drain on the economy as a whole.

Some writers have argued that if the minimum wage is too high, high school students will be tempted to drop out of school to work. For example, R. Morris Coats in an October 4, 1999, article in *Bayou Business Review* argues that a high school junior "may be contemplating quitting school and getting a job. . . . Now think about that young man faced with roughly the same choice, but with 19% more pay per week. . . . The extra $160 a month more is significant [enough] to change his mind." A November 3, 2006, post at EducationTaxCredits makes a similar point: "the immediate income boost that teenage minimum wage earners receive from an increase in the minimum wage is far outweighed by the long term income lost due to forgoing school for work."

Paul Swamidass, writing in 2011 in the *California Journal of Politics and Policy* (vol. 3, no. 1) argues that policy makers must address the problem of the minimum wage level encouraging high school students to drop out. Swamidass says that "we should incentivize high school students to graduate by delaying the statutory minimum wage until high-school graduation. A revised *substandard* minimum wage for those without a valid high school degree should be far lower than the statutory minimum (say, $3, or sufficiently low to serve as a motivator to keep teens in school)." Swamidass argues that dropouts would only be eligible for the regular minimum wage when they reached 25; until then they would receive the lower rate. This policy, he concludes, would motivate teens to graduate, or or get their GED as soon as possible.

In contrast, John Robert Warren and Caitlin Hamrock in a March 2010 article in *Social Forces* argue that there is little evidence linking high school completion to minimum wage. Looking at the impact of changes in state and federal minimum wages for graduating classes from 1982 through 2005, the researchers found "no support for the argument that increasing the minimum wage reduces rates of high school completion." The Stanford newsletter *Pathways* for Winter 2011 notes that Warren and Hamrock's research shows that "we can at least conclude that high schoolers are hardly clamoring to get their hands on minimum wage jobs."

The following viewpoints examine other ways in which the minimum wage affects or is affected by business and the economy.

| "State minimum wage increases have adverse effects on . . . small businesses."

The Minimum Wage Hurts Small Businesses

Joseph J. Sabia

Joseph J. Sabia is a professor of consumer economics at the University of Georgia. In the following viewpoint, he argues that research showing that minimum wage increases do not affect small businesses is faulty. Instead, Sabia says, his research indicates that raising the minimum wage forces small businesses to lay off low-income workers. He notes that in some cases this may actually increase poverty rates. Sabia concludes that other methods, like the Earned Income Tax Credit, are a better way to help workers employed by small businesses.

As you read, consider the following questions:

1. What evidence did Ted Kennedy cite, according to the author, in arguing for an increase in the minimum wage in 2005?

2. According to Sabia, what effect does a 10 percent increase in the minimum wage have on those employed by retail and small businesses?

3. Why does the author say that raising the minimum wage is no longer an effective means of reducing poverty among the working poor?

A recent study by the Fiscal Policy Institute (FPI) (2004) suggests that minimum wage increases do not have adverse employment effects. The authors of the FPI report conclude that states that increased their minimum wages above the federal minimum did not experience declines in small business employment, and, in fact, actually experienced an increase in retail employment. Along with the influential studies of [David] Card et al. and Card and [Alan B.] Krueger, the findings of the FPI study challenge the widely shared view among labor economists that minimum wage hikes cause unemployment of low-skilled workers.

An Important Talking Point

The results of the FPI study have been publicized in the mainstream media (see, for example, New York *Newsday*, [April 3,] 2006) and have been cited by numerous advocates of minimum wage increases at both the federal and state levels. In 2004, Dr. Jared Bernstein, a senior economist at the Economic Policy Institute, testified before the U.S. House Subcommittee on Workforce, Empowerment, and Government Programs. He claimed that a federal minimum wage hike would not have disemployment effects, citing the FPI study's results on retail and small business employment as evidence for his position. Bernstein stated that "between 1998 and 2001, the number of small business establishments grew twice as quickly in states with higher minimum wages (3.1% vs. 1.6%)".

In May 2005, United States Senator Ted Kennedy (D-MA) reintroduced legislation to raise the federal minimum wage from $5.15 to $7.25, and argued that minimum wage increases had no adverse employment effects in the retail industry

History clearly shows that raising the minimum wage has not had any negative impact on jobs, employment, or inflation. In the four years after the last minimum wage increase passed, the economy experienced its strongest growth in over three decades. More than 11 million new jobs were added, at a pace of 232,000 per month. There were ten million new service industry jobs, including more than one and a half million retail jobs, of which nearly 600,000 were restaurant jobs.

Several advocates of state minimum wage hikes have also cited the conclusions of the FPI study. In a legislative analysis of California Senate Bill 1162—which would raise the state minimum wage from $7.25 to $7.75—the Committee on Industrial and Labor Relations bolstered its support for a minimum wage hike by referring to "a recent Fiscal Policy Institute (FPI) study of state minimum wages [that] found no evidence of negative employment effects on small businesses" . . . .

Thus, along with the studies of Card et al. and Card and Krueger, the results of the FPI study have become an important talking point among advocates of state and federal minimum wage hikes. However, there are important theoretical and methodological problems with the FPI report that cast doubt on the conclusion that minimum wage hikes have no adverse effects on retail and small business employment.

Adverse Effects on Employment

This [viewpoint] presents a more careful analysis of the effect of minimum wage hikes during the 1980s, 1990s, and 2000s and finds that there are important adverse employment effects among low-skilled workers in the retail sector and in small businesses. Using Current Population Survey (CPS) data from January 1979 to December 2004, the effect of minimum wage increases on retail and small business employment is estimated. Teenagers are examined as a population of interest because they represent a group of low-skilled workers that are most likely to be directly affected by minimum wage hikes. This [viewpoint] examines the effect of minimum wage increases on the following employment outcomes:

- the share of individuals aged 16–64 employed in the retail industry;
- the share of individuals aged 16–64 employed in small businesses;
- the share of teenagers (age 16–19) employed;
- average hours worked by all teenagers;
- average hours worked by employed teenagers;
- the share of teenagers employed in the retail industry;
- average hours worked by teenagers in the retail industry;
- the share of teenagers employed in small businesses; and
- average hours worked by teenagers in small businesses.

Estimation results suggest consistent evidence of a significant negative relationship between minimum wage increases and retail and small business employment. A 10 percent increase in the minimum wage is associated with a 0.9 to 1.1 percent decline in the share of individuals aged 16–64 who are employed in the retail industry, and a 0.8 to 1.2 percent reduction in the share of individuals aged 16–64 employed in small businesses.

As expected, the effects of minimum wage hikes are larger in magnitude for low-skilled workers. A 10 percent increase in the minimum wage is associated with a 2.7 to 4.3 percent decline in the ratio of teenagers employed in the retail sector, a 5 percent decline in average retail hours worked by all teenagers, and a 2.8 percent decline in retail hours worked by teenagers who remain employed in retail jobs. For small businesses, the disemployment effects are even larger. A 10 percent increase in the minimum wage is associated with a 4.6 to 9.0 percent decline in the ratio of teenagers employed in businesses with 100 or fewer employers, a 4.8 to 8.8 percent decline in average small business hours worked by all teenagers, and a 5.6 to 7.3 percent decline in average small business hours worked by teenagers who remain employed in small businesses.

The[se] results . . . cast doubt on the Fiscal Policy Institute's claim that raising the minimum wage will have no adverse effects on low-skilled employment in retail or small businesses. These findings suggest that state minimum wage increases have adverse effects on employment in retail and small businesses. Moreover, the results suggest that teenagers—a group of low-skilled workers most likely to be adversely affected by minimum wage hikes—experience important declines in employment and hours worked due to minimum wage increases. Taken together with other research by labor economists, this finding suggests that raising the minimum wage is a poor policy tool to aid low-skilled workers. . . .

Negative Effects

This [viewpoint] has examined the impact of minimum wage increases on retail and small business employment, with special attention to employment by a group of low-skilled workers—teenagers—employed in retail and small businesses. These findings provide consistent evidence that minimum wage increases result in a significant decline in retail and small business employment. This finding is robust across several model specifications. A 10 percent increase in state minimum wages is consistently associated with a 1 percent reduction in retail employment and a 1 percent reduction in small business employment.

Minimum wage hikes are associated with an even larger reduction in teenage employment in the retail sector. . . . Moreover, a 10 percent increase in the minimum wage reduces average retail hours worked by 5 percent, and, among teens who remain employed in the retail sector, reduces average hours worked by 2 to 3 percent. Finally, teen employment in small businesses is negatively affected by minimum wage hikes. A 10 percent increase in the minimum wage is associated with a 4.6 to 9.0 percent decline in teenage employment in small businesses and a

"Minimum Wage Increase," cartoon by Alesha Bailey; student journalist, Eastern Illinois University. Reproduced by permission.

4.8 to 8.8 percent reduction in hours worked by teens in the retail sector.

Taken together with other recent work, the[se] findings . . . suggest that low-skilled workers will not escape adverse labor market consequences resulting from minimum wage increases. Moreover, the[se] results . . . suggest that the findings from the Fiscal Policy Institute report (2004) are misleading. Raising the minimum wage has negative effects on the employment and hours worked of low-skilled workers, particularly in the retail sector and in small businesses. This finding is consistent with standard neoclassical economic theory, which suggests that if the price of low-skilled labor rises, employers will reduce the numbers of low-skilled employees, reduce the hours offered to currently employed low-skilled employees, or both.

In addition to the adverse employment effects of the minimum wage, there are other important reasons why raising the minimum wage is a poor policy strategy. Modern-day minimum wage hikes are no longer an effective means of reducing poverty among the working poor. This is true for two reasons. First, most minimum wage workers now live in nonpoor households because they are second or third earners in a family, such as teenage dependents. Second, most workers from poor households earn wage rates higher than the minimum wage. Hence, raising the minimum wage is not target efficient at reducing poverty among the working poor. As [Richard V.] Burkhauser et al. show, the Earned Income Tax Credit (EITC) [a refundable tax credit for families with qualifying children] is a far more effective policy tool to reduce poverty among poor families. Moreover, the EITC has the advantage of avoiding the adverse employment effects described in this study. In fact, [David] Neumark et al. show that a minimum wage hike may actually increase the poverty rate because the increase's adverse effect on hours worked will push nonpoor families into poverty.

The[se] findings . . . should serve as a caution to legislators considering an increase in the minimum wage. While the findings of the FPI study may be seductive to some policymakers, the evidence presented here should serve as a reminder that there is no such thing as a free lunch. Raising the minimum wage will hurt rather than help low-skilled workers in retail and small businesses.

| *"The minimum wage increase . . . is good for business."*

The Minimum Wage Helps Small Businesses

Business for a Fair Minimum Wage

Business for a Fair Minimum Wage is a project of Business for Shared Prosperity, which mobilizes business support for policies that expand opportunity. In the following viewpoint, the organization argues that raising the minimum wage will raise consumer purchasing power and help the economy. The viewpoint also suggests that an increased minimum wage increases worker satisfaction and creates a more stable and productive workforce. The viewpoint also maintains that the minimum wage should be raised in the interest of justice and fairness.

As you read, consider the following questions:

1. Who is Richard Johnson and what reasons does he give for raising the minimum wage, as cited by the author?
2. According to Business for a Fair Minimum Wage, what percentage of workers in Idaho received a raise when the minimum wage was increased in 2009?

3. Why does the author say that the minimum wage was established during the Great Depression?

B usiness owners across the nation are welcoming the July 24 [2009] increase in the federal minimum wage from $6.55 to $7.25. National business leaders and small business owners in states where workers are getting a raise say the increase will boost consumer buying power and promote economic recovery.

Putting Money in the Economy

"A minimum wage increase at this time could be the most important factor in powering our economy out of the recession," said Camille Moran, owner of a paralegal service and Christmas tree farm in Louisiana. "The higher the wage an employee receives, the more income he or she has to purchase goods and services for their family, which is indeed 'the best medicine' for our economy." More than 8% of workers will be affected by the minimum wage increase in Louisiana.

Richard Ketring, president of VHS Cleaning Services in Ashland, Wisc., said, "When we raise the incomes of the lowest paid employees the money is immediately spent and flows instantly into the economy. The increased income can also make for more reliable workers as it reduces the stress that many minimum wage workers experience as they work extra jobs, juggle day care, work when sick or don't receive needed medical care— causing further distress later. I support the minimum wage increase not only because it is the right thing to do, but it is good for business." More than 7% of Wisc. workers will receive a raise.

U.S. Women's Chamber of Commerce CEO Margot Dorfman said, "Now, more than ever, it's imperative that employees are paid a fair minimum wage. It is an unsustainable and dangerous downward spiral to push American workers into poverty and expect taxpayers to pick up the bill for the consequences. Minimum wage laws guarantee to taxpayers that businesses are playing fair and compensating workers at responsible levels."

One out of ten workers will be affected by the minimum wage increase in Texas. "I cannot understand how we expect families to exist without a national wage scale that is a livable wage. Workers' families have to eat too," said Bernard Rapoport, founder and chairman emeritus of American Income Life Insurance Company, headquartered in Waco, TX.

Richard Johnson, president of Associated Merchant Services in Nashville, Tenn. said, "I'm for a higher minimum wage. There is no rational reason why our society should allow some people to earn enough to own five mansions while those who pick their fruit, do their laundry and pick up their garbage can't even afford a small house. Picking fruit and picking up garbage is hard work, and why shouldn't someone who is willing to do that be rewarded with enough income to enjoy a decent lifestyle?" More than 6% of Tenn. workers will get a raise with the minimum wage increase.

Support for a Living Wage

Nearly 1,000 business owners and executives including Costco CEO Jim Sinegal, U.S. Women's Chamber of Commerce CEO Margot Dorfman, ABC Home CEO and 2009 Home Fashion Products Association Retailer of the Year Paulette Cole, Addus Healthcare CEO Mark Heaney, Credo Mobile President Michael Kieschnick, Business Alliance for Local Living Economies Co-Founder Doug Hammond, and small business owners from all 50 states—have signed a statement supporting the minimum wage increase. As the Business For a Fair Minimum Wage statement points out, "Higher wages benefit business by increasing consumer purchasing power, reducing costly employee turnover, raising productivity, and improving product quality, customer satisfaction and company reputation."

With more than 60 local networks in the U.S. representing tens of thousands of locally owned businesses, the Business Alliance for Local Living Economies (BALLE) is the world's fastest growing network of economically and environmentally

Small Businesses Not Hurt

After reviewing the available data, I believe that increasing the minimum wage will help those in need and will not adversely affect small businesses. A 1998 EPI study did not find any significant job loss associated with the 1996–1997 Federal minimum wage increase. On the other hand, the low-wage labor market—i.e. lower unemployment rates and increased average hourly wages—had performed better than in previous years. Small business owners in those states with higher minimum wage rates than the Federal minimum wage rate, such as the State of Washington at $7.93 per hour, appeared to have prospered. The *New York Times* reported on January 11, 2007 that small business owners in Washington's neighboring State of Idaho are hurting because of the State's low minimum wage rate of $5.15 per hour. Many residents living near Washington seek jobs in the Evergreen State, forcing small business owners to offer more than Idaho's minimum wage in order to hire new employees.

Arlen Specter, Congressional Record— Senate, *January 24, 2007.*

sustainable businesses. Michael Shuman, BALLE director of research and public policy, said, "In the view of our members, raising the minimum wage to $7.25 is an overdue step in providing a decent, fair livelihood to American workers and creating a truly 'living economy.'"

"Anyone who thinks the minimum wage shouldn't be raised should try living on it," said Phillip Rubin, CEO of Computer Software for Professionals in Oakland, CA.

"I am a small business owner in Boise, Idaho who strongly supports the increased minimum wage," said Scot McGavin, owner of Puentes Language Programs. "Every person should have enough incentive that investing of themselves in their work will allow them to provide for themselves and their family. This extra income will benefit many in our society since it will be reinvested back into the economy." According to the Economic Policy Institute, nearly 9% of Idaho workers will get a raise when the minimum wage goes up.

Beverly Johnson, legislative chair of Kansas Business and Professional Women said, "We are all in this together. People working hard and responsibly should be paid an amount valuing their personal human dignity. For example, we need 'ditch diggers.' I don't want to dig ditches. If I want my ditches to be dug, then I should not be paying the least amount that a 'desperate' person will work for. I must pay fairly in a way that will assure he can afford necessities and preserve his human dignity—even if it means I earn a little less." More than 8% of Kansas workers will receive a raise.

"It's a myth that a minimum wage increase kills job development," said Lya Sorano, founder of Atlanta Women in Business. "To get out of this recession, we need more money to circulate. That happens when people get bigger paychecks, who today can't afford to buy the goods and services they need—goods and services from some of the same people who seem to be opposed to the increase." Nearly 7% of workers will see a raise in Georgia.

"The stress of poverty puts the mind in a place of worry instead of work," said Nancy Denker, owner of Focus Ink in Albuquerque, NM. "Living on a shoestring is not the best incentive for workers. Business owners must realize that as our community prospers, so will business."

A Stronger Foundation

The first federal minimum wage was legislated during the Great Depression to boost wages to ease the hardship of workers and increase the consumer purchasing power needed for job creation and economic recovery. With the economy in the worst crisis since the Depression, the minimum wage increase plays the same role today. Business leaders say that putting a stronger wage floor under workers will put a stronger foundation under our economy and our country.

"History has proven time and again that increasing the minimum wage increases purchasing power among people who are living hand to mouth and must therefore spend the additional income on necessities—food, clothing, transportation and so on," said Arnold Hiatt, chairman of the Stride Rite Foundation and former CEO of the Stride Rite Corporation. "What better way to increase demand for the goods and services that businesses urgently need."

The minimum wage was not increased for ten years from 1997 to 2007—the longest period in history without a raise. Even with the raise to $7.25, workers will still make less than the $7.93 they made in 1956, adjusting for inflation.

Miranda Magagnini, Co-Ceo of IceStone, the award-winning Brooklyn, NY–based manufacturer of sustainable durable surfaces, said, "We pay living wages at IceStone plus medical benefits because we do not believe folks can 'live' on minimum wage—especially without health insurance. A raise in the minimum is a move in the right direction, but $7.25 an hour is $2.75 lower than it should be."

"We cannot build a strong 21st century economy on a 1950s' wage floor. We cannot build a strong 21st century economy when more and more hardworking Americans struggle to make ends meet," business leaders say in the statement at www .businessforafairminimumwage.org. "A fair minimum wage is a sound investment in the future of our communities and our nation."

"A fair minimum wage protects the middle class and gives entry level workers some economic breathing room," said Lew Prince, CEO and co-owner of Vintage Vinyl in St. Louis, MO. "When everyone is feeling insecure, rebuilding our economy starts with showing hard-working Americans that their time has value and their work will be rewarded. If we want to put the great American success story back on track, all of us need to feel that we have access to that opportunity."

> "[The corner store], not Wal-Mart, will
> suffer if Congress raises the minimum
> wage [because then] . . . Wal-Mart has
> one fewer competitor."

Increasing the Minimum Wage Favors Megastores Like Wal-Mart

Timothy P. Carney

Timothy P. Carney is a columnist for the Washington Examiner *and the author of* The Big Ripoff: How Big Government and Big Business Steal Your Money. *In the following viewpoint, he argues that large discount stores like Wal-Mart and Costco buy in such bulk that they get lower prices and can thus afford to pay their employees more than a minimum wage. Smaller businesses, he says, have to hire workers at lower salaries. A hike in the minimum wage would hurt small businesses, Carney maintains, and so Wal-Mart and Costco support an increased minimum wage in order to hurt their competitors.*

As you read, consider the following questions:

1. Why does Carney say that it is unlikely that the mini-

mum-wage hike would help Wal-Mart customers buy more goods?

2. According to the author, how much does Wal-Mart pay its entry-level workers?

3. Who are Paulette Cole and Eileen Fisher, and why does Carney say that it makes sense for them to support a minimum-wage hike?

A mid all those goodies in the Iraq [war] supplemental funding bill [of 2007] for sugar beet farmers, California orange growers and ornamental shrub dealers lies another provision requested by big business: an increase in the federal minimum wage.

Helping Big Businesses Hurt Competitors

Two of the five biggest retailers in the U.S.—Wal-Mart and Costco—have lobbied for the minimum-wage hike that Democrats are now on the verge of delivering, a move that would likely help the discount giants by hurting their smaller competitors.

Wal-Mart is the largest retailer in the world, and a favorite bad guy for labor unions, anti-sprawl activists and anti-corporate crusaders, among others. One prominent critic of Wal-Mart is the AFL-CIO labor organization, which has multiple Web sites dedicated to assailing the company's treatment of workers.

The Web site of one AFL-CIO spin-off features a parody cartoon with a [country music star] Garth Brooks sound-alike singing "I've got friends with low wages." Another AFL-CIO anti-Wal-Mart Web page declares, "Wal-Mart kills family retail businesses."

Ironically, the one issue where Wal-Mart and the AFL-CIO are on the same side—that the minimum wage should be hiked— could be one of the most serious threats to Wal-Mart's Mom and Pop competitors.

Top 20 Retailers, 2010

Rank	Company	2009 Sales (000)
1	Wal-Mart	$304,939,000
2	Kroger	$76,733,000
3	Target	$63,435,000
4	Walgreen	$63,335,000
5	The Home Depot	$59,176,000
6	Costco	$56,548,000
7	CVS Caremark	$55,355,000
8	Lowe's	$47,220,000
9	Sears Holdings	$44,043,000
10	Best Buy	$37,314,000
11	Safeway	$34,980,000
12	SUPERVALU	$31,637,000
13	Rite Aid	$25,669,000
14	Publix	$24,515,000
15	Macy's	$23,489,000
16	Ahold USA	$22,825,000
17	McDonald's	$22,240,000
18	Delhaize America	$18,994,000
19	J.C. Penney	$17,556,000
20	Kohl's	$17,178,000

TAKEN FROM: Stores, "2010 Top 100 Retailers," July 2010. www
.stores.org.

In October 2005, in an address to his employees, Wal-Mart CEO Lee Scott called on Congress "to take a responsible look at the minimum wage," saying, "the U.S. minimum wage of $5.15 an hour has not been raised in nearly a decade, and we believe it is out of date with the times."

Since then, Scott has become even more explicit in his public calls for a higher minimum wage. His official reason is that his "customers simply don't have the money to buy basic necessities between paychecks." This is unlikely, given demographic studies that show very little overlap between minimum-wage workers and Wal-Mart customers.

A 2004 survey by Mediamark Research found that 73 percent of Wal-Mart shoppers own their homes. The same study found that a vast majority of Wal-Mart shoppers are 25 years old or older (59 percent are between ages 25 and 54. The survey didn't indicate what percentage were over 54 years old), while data from the Bureau of Labor Statistics (BLS) indicate that 53 percent of minimum-wage workers were under 25 in 2005.

BLS statistics suggest a more likely reason to expect Wal-Mart to benefit from a higher minimum wage: After leisure and hospitality (mostly restaurants and hotels), the industry whose workers are most likely to earn minimum wage is the retail trade industry.

Raising minimum wage would disproportionately affect the retail sector—but not Wal-Mart, which pays entry-level workers at least $8 an hour. The average wages for full-time hourly Wal-Mart employees, of course, is higher.

John Doe Will Suffer

John Doe's Corner Store, meanwhile, might hire a high school kid for nights and weekends at $5.15 or $6 per hour. John Doe, not Wal-Mart, will suffer if Congress raises the minimum wage. When the corner store goes out of business, Wal-Mart has one fewer competitor for customers, supplies, employees and real estate.

It's another illustration of an important economic reality: Regulation adds to overhead, which serves as a barrier to entry and disproportionately affects smaller businesses. Of course, not only small business, but also some major retailers, including Home Depot and Kroger, will be affected by a minimum-wage hike.

Businesses supporting an increase in the minimum wage have formed a coalition called Business for a Fair Minimum Wage, whose Web site features a public petition by businesses for a minimum-wage hike. The most prominent signatory is Costco, which, like Wal-Mart, has such economies of scale that it can pay higher wages than smaller retailers and still undercut them on prices.

Costco CEO Jim Sinegal (who has donated about $400,000 to Democratic politicians over the years, and none to Republicans) said in a press release from the coalition, "The increase in the minimum wage is long overdue."

Just below Sinegal's name on the wage-hike petition are Paulette Cole, who sells high-end furnishings, and Eileen Fisher, who designs expensive clothes. Both of these employers pay workers well, and pass that cost onto their well-heeled customers. An increased minimum wage would not affect them.

Senate versions of the minimum-wage hike were tied to tax provisions—both tax cuts and tax increases—that were not in the corresponding House measures. The tax measures affect executive pay and depreciation among other issues, and they seem to favor small businesses. It is unclear whether they will end up in the final minimum-wage legislation, which will likely pass whether or not that legislation is included in the Iraq war funding bill.

> "[Wal-Mart] was willing to break the
> law to avoid paying the minimum
> wage."

Wal-Mart Historically Has Fought Increases in the Minimum Wage

Harold Meyerson

Harold Meyerson is the editor at large of the American Prospect *and a columnist for the* Washington Post. *In the following viewpoint he argues that Wal-Mart has a long-standing opposition to fair treatment for its workers, starting with founder Sam Walton's die-hard opposition to the minimum wage. Meyerson says that Wal-Mart's business model is based on low prices and low wages, and that it could not exist without the large income disparities in the US economy. He concludes that Wal-Mart has helped to remake the US economy for the worse.*

As you read, consider the following questions:

1. According to Meyerson, how did Sam Walton initially attempt to evade the minimum wage?
2. What aspects of business does the author say that Walton

revolutionized?

3. What countries has Wal-Mart had little success in, and why is this true, according to Meyerson?

The story isn't part of the official Wal-Mart creation epic, but it tells us almost all we need to know about the company's approach to the interests of its employees and the laws of the nation. Around the time that the young Sam Walton opened his first stores, John Kennedy redeemed a presidential campaign promise by persuading Congress to extend the minimum wage to retail workers, who had until then not been covered by the law. Congress granted an exclusion, however, to small businesses with annual sales beneath $1 million—a figure that in 1965 it lowered to $250,000.

Walton was furious. The mechanization of agriculture had finally reached the backwaters of the Ozark Plateau, where he was opening one store after another. The men and women who had formerly worked on small farms suddenly found themselves redundant, and he could scoop them up for a song, as little as 50 cents an hour. Now the goddamn federal government was telling him he had to pay his workers the $1.15 hourly minimum. Walton's response was to divide up his stores into individual companies whose revenues didn't exceed the $250,000 threshold. Eventually, though, a federal court ruled that this was simply a scheme to avoid paying the minimum wage, and he was ordered to pay his workers the accumulated sums he owed them, plus a double-time penalty thrown in for good measure.

Wal-Mart cut the checks, but Walton also summoned the employees at a major cluster of his stores to a meeting. "I'll fire anyone who cashes the check," he told them.

Besides its Dickensian shock value, this story—told by Nelson Lichtenstein in his book about Wal-Mart—points to a phenomenon of wider significance. The company that was willing to break the law to avoid paying the minimum wage is now the largest private-sector employer in the nation and the world, with

1.4 million employees in the United States and 2 million overall, more than 6,000 stores, and revenues that exceed those of Target, Home Depot, Sears, Kmart, Safeway, and Kroger—combined. By virtue of its size and its mastery of logistics, Wal-Mart is able to demand low prices from its thousands of suppliers and thus inflict low wages on their employees. Its low prices have also forced reductions in wages and benefits at the unionized supermarkets with which it threatens to compete.

As the unionized General Motors was big enough to set the pattern for the employment of nonprofessional Americans in the three decades following World War II, Wal-Mart is now so big it is setting the pattern today. Each created a distinct national buying public for its goods that was far larger than its immediate work force: in GM's case, workers who could afford to buy new cars; in Wal-Mart's, workers who could afford to shop nowhere except Wal-Mart. With Wal-Mart's rise, the same traditional values that underpinned Sam Walton's cheating and threatening of his workers—contempt for Yankee laws and regulations, and a preference for the authoritarian, low-wage labor system of the South—have become more the norm than the exception in America's economic life.

For the past year, Americans have focused, and understandably so, on the ways in which Wall Street has misshaped the American economy, how finance has grown large over the past 20 years as manufacturing has shrunk. But the rise of finance is just half the story; it takes the rise of retail to complete the tale. Both Wall Street and Wal-Mart played a central role in the deindustrialization of the United States: 40,000 U.S factories were closed between 2001, when China was admitted to the World Trade Organization, and 2007, during which years Wal-Mart's Chinese imports tripled in value from $9 billion to $27 billion.

The rise of Wal-Mart, and the national economy it has shaped in its image, is a story that Lichtenstein, a professor of history at the University of California, Santa Barbara, is eminently suited to tell. He's also the author of *The Most Dangerous Man in Detroit,* a biography of United Auto Workers President Walter Reuther that is one of the definitive accounts of the rise of the unionized, high-wage, mid-20th-century economy that Wal-Mart has done so much to destroy. *The Retail Revolution* now tells the story of how Walton, strongly abetted by Ronald Reagan, pulled down the world that Reuther, strongly abetted by Franklin Roosevelt, created. It is not the definitive scholarly history that Lichtenstein's Reuther biography is, but it is surely the best account we have of Wal-Mart's metamorphosis from a backwater chain to the nation's dominant corporation, and it contains more direct reporting than is normally found in the works of historians. The story of Walton's minimum-wage evasion came from Lichtenstein's interviews with former Wal-Mart executives.

Lichtenstein's account of Wal-Mart's rise isn't uniformly negative. Walton and his top lieutenants, following in the footsteps of such American economic icons as Henry Ford, can point to hugely important business innovations that stand alongside their social primitivism. As Ford revolutionized production, so Walton revolutionized distribution and logistics—the business of getting the product from the plant to the store in the fastest, cheapest, most efficient way possible. Well before other retailers, he understood the potential of the barcode for tracking the supply and demand for products. He changed warehouses from giant storage rooms to distribution centers where products arriving from ports or plants were turned around and delivered to stores within a day. He invested in more computer technology and communications satellites than his rivals, and developed better data on which goods moved and how best to sell them than their manufacturers (even venerable firms like Procter & Gamble) possessed. Once Wal-Mart became America's retail giant, he compelled suppliers like P&G to seek Wal-Mart's approval for new products and its help in crafting them. The data also enabled Wal-Mart to manage its stores from its corporate headquarters in Bentonville, Arkansas, reducing store managers to foremen under constant pressure to sell more and spend less.

But Wal-Mart's distinctive identity came from fusing its brilliant use of new technology with its rigorous adherence to the old exploitative Southern labor practices. The Southern traditionalism of Walton and his lieutenants dictated that the stores' managers would be men and its salesclerks women, and no federal statute or class-action lawsuit has been able to dethrone that tradition yet. Wal-Mart is also famously, pathologically anti-union, but its antipathy toward its nonunion work force is no less remarkable. The firm prohibits overtime pay (even before the current recession, the average Wal-Mart employee worked 34 hours a week), offers health-insurance plans that fewer than 50 percent of its U.S. workers opt to purchase (the most common plan contains a $3,000 annual family deductible, a great deal of money for workers making a little more than the minimum wage), and keeps its labor costs down to 10 percent of sales, in contrast to levels of 11 percent to 13 percent for its discount retail competitors.

Annual turnover among employees is huge—40 percent in most recent years, though in the late 1990s, when unemployment was low, it reached a staggering 70 percent. Wal-Mart seldom discharges employees, an act that would require it to pay penalties if the government found a pattern of excessive firings. Rather, it simply gives its workers such unwieldy schedules and such impossible work loads that quitting, like low prices, is an everyday constant. So, as Lichtenstein documents, is employee theft—a problem that Wal-Mart addressed by locking in its night shifts until public exposure brought that practice to an end.

Wal-Mart has succeeded brilliantly throughout the NAFTA nations. It has become the biggest retailer in both Canada and Mexico (and it staved off unionization of its Canadian stores by closing down the one whose workers voted to go union). But it had to withdraw from Germany, where the laws regulating hours and wages made its normal business practices impossible, and has also fared poorly in Japan. As Lichtenstein notes, in nations such as Germany and Japan, where high disposable incomes are

The Importance of Wal-Mart and Retail

When [business newsmagazine] *Fortune* inserted retailers on its list of giant corporations [in the 1990s], Wal-Mart immediately popped up as number 4, measured by sales revenue, right behind GM, Ford, and Exxon Mobil. Sears, Roebuck was number 9 and Kmart number 15. Indeed, by 1995 sixteen of the top one hundred firms on the Fortune 500 list were mass retailers. Wal-Mart, which also displaced General Motors as the largest private employer in the nation, moved to number 1 on the Fortune 500 list in 2002, and it has held that rank ever since, except for the year 2006 when the spike in oil prices put Exxon Mobil at the top. Today, the retail trade employs some 15.5 million workers, more than in all manufacturing. Wal-Mart alone employs almost twenty times the number of workers as the biggest oil company.

Nelson Lichtenstein, The Retail Revolution: How Wal-Mart Created a Brave New World of Business, *2009.*

"shared relatively equally throughout the population, Wal-Mart's EDLP [Every Day Low Prices] policy is not so much of a trump card." Wal-Mart's efforts in Germany were not helped by the fact that its policy of encouraging workers to call in anonymously to report on misdeeds (including union sentiments) of their fellow workers reminded Germans of the late, unlamented Stasi.

Wal-Mart's more serious failure of market penetration remains its inability to break into America's major coastal cities or Chicago. There, the specter of its superstores—stores that include supermarkets, whose success has already given Wal-Mart

30 percent of the U.S. retail food market—poses a direct threat to unionized supermarket workers. In 2003, Southern California supermarkets, after decades of mutually profitable labor relations, told the United Food and Commercial Workers that they would have to reduce wages and benefits to compete with Wal-Mart, and, after breaking the union's strike, imposed a contract in which new hires were offered not the traditional health insurance package but one modeled on Wal-Mart's. At the time, the proportion of Southern California grocery workers with health insurance stood at 94 percent; by 2007, it had declined to 54 percent.

After that defeat, the unions and its allies fought back, convincing city councils and governmental agencies in big East Coast and California cities to use zoning ordinances and bans on big-box stores to keep Wal-Mart out of town. Public indignation over the company's labor practices has also contributed to its inability to enter blue-state markets.

With its stock price stagnant for nearly a decade due in part to its failure to expand to blue-state America, and with Democrats now in control in Washington, Wal-Mart is currently undergoing a great cosmetic makeover. It has announced it will develop a green profile for all the products it sells and has even proclaimed its support for an employer mandate in any emerging health-reform package. What it is not willing to relinquish is its die-hard opposition to unions and labor-law reform, its existential commitment to the Southern model of labor relations. Wal-Mart cannot thrive in a nation where prosperity is broadly shared, and it will do all it can to keep that from happening.

That Wal-Mart has been waylaid in part by the political expression of indignant consumers should come as no surprise to readers of Lawrence Glickman's *Buying Power: A History of Consumer Activism in America*. As Glickman, a history professor at the University of South Carolina, makes clear, Americans have a long, if largely forgotten, history of supporting political causes by withdrawing their patronage from certain stores or products—including efforts by abolitionists to establish stores that sold clothing free from the taint of plantation cotton, and by Southern slavers to boycott products made in the North. Of particular interest are the efforts that Glickman has uncovered of urban Southern blacks to resist the coming of Jim Crow by boycotting newly segregated municipal streetcar lines at the turn of the century—including a Montgomery, Alabama, streetcar boycott 55 years before Rosa Parks sat down in one of the front seats of a Montgomery bus.

But it is one thing for Glickman to rescue these campaigns from history's dustbin and quite another for him to give them an importance that most of them do not deserve. In the battles for the abolitions of slavery, for worker rights and for civil rights, the actions of sympathetic consumers seldom amounted to more than a sideshow. Glickman sometimes makes too much of them, and whehen he turns hisattention to the battle for consumer rights during the 1960s and 1970s, he accords it a centrality that other historians of the time have trouble recognizing. Ignoring the pivotal role that the politics of race played in the demise of the mid-20th-century Democratic majority, he writes that "Great Society liberalism was defeated in large measure because of tis association with consumerism." What we learn from this assessment is that Glickman may have been immersed in this topic for too many years.

> "Minimum-wage laws . . . infringe the
> right of an employer and an employee
> to make whatever wage agreement they
> choose."

The Minimum Wage Is an Unethical Infringement of Economic Freedom

Laurence M. Vance

Laurence M. Vance is a writer and an adjunct instructor in ac-counting and economics at Pensacola Junior College in Pensacola, Florida. In the following viewpoint, he argues that minimum-wage laws increase unemployment. He also says that such laws are an unethical interference by the government in the economy. He says minimum-wage regulations infringe the right to make free labor contracts. Minimum-wage laws, he concludes, are not only harmful but unethical, and all of them should be abolished.

As you read, consider the following questions:

1. Why did workers in the state of Florida receive a pay raise in May 2005, according to Vance?
2. According to the author, what is the bottom line argument

Laurence M. Vance, "Minimum Wage, Maximum Intervention," *Freedom Daily*, November-December 2005. Copyright © 2005 by The Future of Freedom Foundation. All rights reserved. Reproduced by permission. www.fff.org.

of supporters of the minimum wage?

3. What does Vance suggest an employee should do if he or she can't make ends meet on the minimum wage?

M any workers in my state of Florida received a pay raise this past May [2005]. No, Floridians did not suddenly become more productive and demand a salary increase because they are now more valuable to their employers. And no, Florida businesses did not suddenly become more profitable and decide to share their good fortune with their employees.

Voting for Wage Increases

The reason many workers in Florida received a pay raise is that they voted for it. The new Section 24 in Article X of the Florida Constitution annually and permanently raises the minimum wage in the state of Florida. It resulted from a constitutional amendment approved by Florida voters back on November 2, 2004. There are actually seven paragraphs (a–g) in Section 24 regarding the minimum-wage increase. Paragraph (c) contains the substance of the new requirement:

> Employers shall pay Employees Wages no less than the Minimum Wage for all hours worked in Florida. Six months after enactment, the Minimum Wage shall be established at an hourly rate of $6.15. On September 30th of that year and on each following September 30th, the state Agency for Workforce Innovation shall calculate an adjusted Minimum Wage rate by increasing the current Minimum Wage rate by the rate of inflation during the twelve months prior to each September 1st using the consumer price index for urban wage earners and clerical workers, CPI-W, or a successor index as calculated by the United States Department of Labor. Each adjusted Minimum Wage rate calculated shall be published and take effect on the following January 1st. For tipped Employees meeting eligibility requirements for the tip credit under the FLSA

[Fair Labor Standards Act], Employers may credit towards satisfaction of the Minimum Wage tips up to the amount of the allowable FLSA tip credit in 2003.

What Florida voters saw on their ballots is this summary of the amendment:

This amendment creates a Florida minimum wage covering all employees in the state covered by the federal minimum wage. The state minimum wage will start at $6.15 per hour six months after enactment, and thereafter be indexed to inflation each year. It provides for enforcement, including double damages for unpaid wages, attorney's fees, and fines by the state. It forbids retaliation against employees for exercising this right. The impact of this amendment on costs and revenues of state and local governments is expected to be minimal.

What is missing from this summary is the amendment's impact on the businesses that pay some of their employees the minimum wage as well as its impact on unskilled workers trying to find employment. One does not have to be an economist to see the detrimental effects of minimum-wage legislation. An increase in the minimum wage will increase a business's labor costs.

It doesn't matter if anyone thinks that businesses exploit their workers and should pay them all a higher wage because they can "afford it." It is an undeniable fact that their labor costs will go up. And if a business's costs increase, that business's profits will go down unless it can offset its increased costs by raising prices, lowering expenses, increasing productivity, or making use of some combination of the three. If a reduction in profit cannot be offset by any of these measures, then a business can go out of business, live with a lower profit margin, or stagnate because of a lack of funds to expand its operations. The minimum wage causes unemployment because it prices unskilled workers out of the market.

State and Federal Minimum Wage

Florida voters probably also did not realize that up until the passage of this amendment, Florida had no minimum-wage law. In fact, the states of Alabama, Arizona, Louisiana, Mississippi, South Carolina, and Tennessee currently do not have a minimum-wage law. There are also two states with a minimum wage that is less than the federal minimum: Kansas ($2.65) and Ohio ($4.25).

This does not mean that employers in states with no minimum wage can pay their employees Third World wages. The federal minimum wage of $5.15 an hour applies to any employee in any state who is covered by the FLSA [Fair Labor Standards Act]. And according to the U.S. Department of Labor,

> All employees of certain enterprises having workers engaged in interstate commerce, producing goods for interstate commerce, or handling, selling, or otherwise working on goods or materials that have been moved in or produced for such commerce by any person are covered by FLSA.

The FLSA basically applies to everyone in the United States because employees of firms that are not covered enterprises under FLSA still may be subject to its minimum-wage, overtime-pay, and child-labor provisions if they are individually engaged in interstate commerce or in the production of goods for interstate commerce or in any closely related process or occupation directly essential to such production. Such employees include those who work in communications or transportation; regularly use the mails, telephones, or telegraph for interstate communication or keep records of interstate transactions; handle, ship, or receive goods moving in interstate commerce; regularly cross state lines in the course of employment; or work for independent employers who contract to do clerical, custodial, maintenance, or other work for firms engaged in interstate commerce or in the production of goods for interstate commerce.

The reason Florida can raise its minimum wage is that the FLSA also permits states and cities to set their minimum wage higher than the federal minimum. In this case, the state minimum trumps the federal minimum. So, in addition to Florida, the following states have a minimum wage that is higher than the federal minimum: Alaska ($7.15), California ($6.75), Connecticut ($7.10), Delaware ($6.15), Hawaii ($6.25), Illinois ($6.50), Maine ($6.35), Massachusetts ($6.75), New York ($6.00), Oregon ($7.25), Rhode Island ($6.75), Vermont ($7.00), and Washington ($7.35). The rate in the District of Columbia ($6.60) is also above the federal minimum. And also like Florida, the District of Columbia and the states of Illinois, New York, Oregon, Vermont, and Washington just raised their minimum wage this year [2005].

Increases in state minimum-wage rates are destined to continue. The new Florida minimum-wage law also contains an indexing provision. This means that Florida joins Oregon and Washington as the only states to index their minimum wage to inflation. The minimum wage is already scheduled to increase in New York to $6.75 in 2006 and $7.15 in 2007. New Jersey is increasing its minimum wage to $7.15 by October of 2006. Movements are also under way in Hawaii, Pennsylvania, New Hampshire, and Minnesota to boost their state's minimu wage.

Because of agitation by "living-wage" advocates such as the Association of Community Organizations for Reform Now (ACORN), some cities and counties have passed living-wage ordinances that raise the minimum wage within their jurisdiction. The city of Sonoma, California, recently mandated that "covered" employers pay a minimum of $11.70 an hour with health benefits or $13.20 without health benefits, indexed annually to the consumer price index. There are today about 125 cities and counties with living-wage ordinances.

Origins of the Minimum Wage

The minimum wage began as part of the Fair Labor Standards Act (FLSA) of 1938. Along with the Davis-Bacon Act and the National Labor Relations (Wagner) Act, the FLSA is one of the three major pieces of New Deal employment legislation that survive today. The original FLSA curtailed child labor, set the maximum work week at 44 hours, and established a minimum wage of 25 cents an hour.

That's right. There was no federal minimum wage in the United States until 1938. Since the turn of the century the states had sought to regulate child labor, the hours in the work day, and overtime pay, but in *Adkins v. Children's Hospital* (1923), the Supreme Court ruled that a minimum-wage law passed in the District of Columbia was "an unconstitutional interference with the freedom of contract included within the guaranties of the Due Process clause of the Fifth Amendment." The Court concluded that there was a fundamental difference between regulating hours and regulating the rate of pay. But a few years later, in the case of *West Coast Hotel v. Parrish* (1937), this ruling was overturned when the Court upheld a Washington state law setting a minimum wage for women. This prepared the way for Congress to pass a federal minimum wage law.

The work week was lowered to 40 hours in 1945, where it remains today, and the minimum wage has been raised 18 times, with the last increase [as of 2005] being in 1997.

All arguments for the minimum wage come down to this: since no family can survive on an income lower than the minimum wage, it is the job of government to mandate a minimum wage to keep people out of poverty. No matter how elaborate the argument, this is the bottom line.

Even if that were a true statement it would still not be a valid argument for the minimum wage. If someone can't support a family on his salary, then he should not have a family until he has a higher salary. It is not the fault of business or society that an unskilled and uneducated worker decides to have a family and then finds out that he can't make ends meet. Moreover, why should the person who is giving him a job be forced to fund his excess expenses? Indeed, why should anyone be forced to do so?

The case against the minimum wage from an economic standpoint has been made many times. It increases the price of goods and services, since it raises employers' costs. It limits economic growth by increasing the cost of labor. And because it raises employment barriers for the unskilled and uneducated, it causes unemployment. As the Austrian economist Murray Rothbard (1926—1995) explains,

> In truth, there is only one way to regard a minimum wage law: it is compulsory unemployment, period. The law says: it is illegal, and therefore criminal, for anyone to hire anyone else below the level of X dollars an hour. This means, plainly and simply, that a large number of free and voluntary wage contracts are now outlawed and hence that there will be a large amount of unemployment. Remember that the minimum wage law provides no jobs; it only outlaws them; and outlawed jobs are the inevitable result.

If raising the minimum wage will truly lift people out of poverty and not lead to unemployment, then why raise it only a dollar or two? That still won't be enough for the typical family of four to make ends meet. Why not raise it to $12.50 an hour, as the Green Party advocated in its 2000 party platform? Why not just mandate that every employee is to be paid a minimum of $50 an hour? That would give everyone an income high enough that the government could end all transfer-payment programs. The trouble with a $50 per hour minimum wage is that the government could end all transfer payment programs but one—unemployment compensation. Massive unemployment would result from such a draconian increase in the minimum wage, as Rothbard again explains:

> It is obvious that the minimum wage advocates do not pursue their own logic, because if they push it to such heights, virtually the entire labor force will be disemployed. In short, *you*

can have as much unemployment as you want, simply by pushing the legally minimum wage high enough.

But if raising the minimum wage is bad economics, why is
there always agitation for its increase? The answer is that raising the minimum wage has everything to do with politics and
nothing to do with economics. If the members of Congress really
wanted to help the economy, they would adopt a laissez-faire approach to the economy instead of an interventionist one.

Naturally, those who are looking for an entry-level job, those
who are currently making the minimum wage, and those who
make more than the minimum wage but stand to benefit from
its increase—as long as they can get a job, keep a job, or receive
a wage increase that keeps up with an increase in prices—are
happy to see any increase in the minimum wage regardless of the
consequences. And so are the politicians in Congress, who are
trying to pick up votes while they pander to the numerous "antipoverty" special-interest groups.

Philosophical and Pragmatic Arguments

In addition to the economic arguments, there are also philosophical and pragmatic arguments against the minimum wage.

First, all minimum-wage laws are based on the fallacy that
selling one's labor on the market is something special compared
with selling one's goods on the market. This Marxian fixation on
the primacy of labor cannot overthrow the fact that the price of
labor is ultimately determined by the forces of supply and demand, just like the price of anything else.

Second, if minimum-wage laws are needed to "protect" employees, then why aren't minimum prices needed to "protect"
employers? If the government is going to establish a floor under
which wages cannot fall, then why not a floor under which prices
of goods cannot fall? Why doesn't the state just set minimum
prices for everything? Unless one subscribes to the primacy-of-

labor fallacy, this is the logical conclusion. This, of course, would be absurd. Can you imagine a store having to keep track of the minimum prices on a bar of soap, a pack of gum, a loaf of bread, and a can of peas—along with 50,000 other items?

Third, the making of minimum-wage laws by the government, whether federal, state, or local, means that the government must be able to determine the "correct" or "just" price for labor. But if the government can determine the "correct" or "just" price for labor, then it must also be able to determine the proper price of everything else. Allowing the state to intervene in the labor market merely opens the door for the state to intervene in every other market. Intervention begets more intervention.

Fourth, minimum-wage laws advance the notion that the government is responsible for our well-being and prosperity.

Fifth, all minimum-wage laws are based on the myth that businesses will exploit their workers without such laws. Supporters of the minimum wage act as though people would still be working for less than the original 25-cent-an-hour minimum wage without government intervention. But if businesses will exploit their workers without the minimum wage, then why do so many people make well above the minimum wage? Why can't businesses just force people to work for the minimum wage? The theory of the exploitation of labor is the foundation of Marxism and has no place in a capitalist society.

Sixth, minimum-wage laws are egalitarian because they foster the notion that everyone should be paid the same regardless of the employee's ability or the employer's benevolence.

Seventh, minimum-wage laws imply that everyone has a right to a "living wage." Everyone has the freedom to work or not work in whatever industry he chooses. Everyone also has the freedom to get or not get the necessary education or skills to obtain a good-paying job. But no one has the right to anything beyond what he and his employer agree to. If someone can't "make it" on the minimum wage, he has a variety of options: find a better job, take a second job, send a family member to work, get the necessary education or skills to obtain a good-paying job, or simply work hard and get promoted out of the minimum-wage job.

Sure, entry-level workers at McDonald's make the minimum wage, but McDonald's needs managers too, and it doesn't require a college degree. And who is more qualified to be a manager than someone who has worked his way up through the ranks? There is an imperative to work and strive to better one's self, but there is no right to a "living wage."

Freedom of Contract

And finally, minimum-wage laws violate freedom of contract. They infringe the right of an employer and an employee to make whatever wage agreement they choose. This is what is done with most aspects of employment. According to the U.S. Department of Labor,

> While FLSA [the Fair Labor Standards Act] does set basic minimum wage and overtime pay standards and regulates the employment of minors, there are a number of employment practices which FLSA does not regulate. For example, FLSA does not require: vacation, holiday, severance, or sick pay; meal or rest periods, holidays off, or vacations; premium pay for weekend or holiday work; pay raises or fringe benefits; and a discharge notice, reason for discharge, or immediate payment of final wages to terminated employees. Also, FLSA does not limit the number of hours in a day or days in a week an employee may be required or scheduled to work, including overtime hours, if the employee is at least 16 years old.

The U.S. Department of Labor says about the things the FLSA doesn't require, "The above matters are for agreement between the employer and the employees or their authorized representatives." That statement says a mouthful, for it is exactly the way things ought to be—for every aspect of employment. There is no good reason that what the government says about these things ought not to apply to wages as well.

The solution is obviously to abolish all minimum-wage laws, whether federal, state, county, or city.

If you thought that the Republicans in Congress were conservatives who favored limited government intervention in the economy—think again. Republicans are not at all averse to raising the minimum wage—as long as their plan is adopted. A recent proposal by Senate Democrats to raise the minimum wage to $7.25 in three increments over 26 months garnered the support of only four Republicans.

But a Republican plan to increase the minimum wage to $6.25 over 18 months received the support of 38 Republicans. Sen. Rick Santorum (R-Pa.), the author of the Republican proposal, was quoted as saying, "I have not had any ideological problem with the minimum wage." This vote and this quotation show that the only difference between the Republicans and the Democrats when it comes to the minimum wage is the amount and the timing of its increase.

It is unfortunate that the party responsible for the minimum wage (the Congress) is also the only party that can abolish the minimum wage. Therefore, it is the members of Congress *and* their constituents who must be educated in the philosophy of liberty—a liberty that includes absolute freedom of contract when it comes to employment.

*"Assault on the minimum wage is ... an
assault on the economy of the United
States of America."*

The Attack on the Minimum Wage Is an Unethical Assault on the Economy

Stephen Herrington

*Stephen Herrington is a retired engineer for Symantec, Visicorp,
and Apple Computer. In the following viewpoint, he argues that
the minimum wage is vital for the economy. He says that business
and labor are in a constant struggle—the former to lower wages,
the latter to raise them. Government, he says, should balance this
struggle so workers have enough resources to buy goods and drive
the economy. Minimum wage, he says, is an important way to protect workers' buying power and thus the economy. Business opposition to minimum wage is therefore short-sighted and ultimately
unethical.*

As you read, consider the following questions:

1. According to Herrington, what is the cornerstone of
   economics?

2. What does the author say the southern states hoped to do with the Tenth Amendment to the Constitution?

3. In 1968 what was the minimum wage, and what does Herrington say one could support on it?

There comes a time, every few years actually, when government has to be the mommy of all the little greedy business boys and girls and make them take their medicine. Among the medications that business most dislikes the taste of is the Minimum Wage. Because business dislikes it, the GOP [Republican Party] dislikes it, joined at the hip as they are to business.

Minimum Wage Maintains Order

Joe Miller, the crackpot Tea Party[1] loon that won the GOP nomination for the Senate from Alaska recently said, in public, that he thought the minimum wage to be unconstitutional. Bear in mind that the entire GOP hates the minimum wage. They stalled increases in it for the entire [George W.] Bush Administration. Even more mainstream GOP candidates like Dino Rossi, Senate candidate in Washington State, have argued to lower it, although on less obviously irrational grounds than its constitutionality. Both Joe Miller and Dino are irretrievably wrong.

Rossi argues that minimum wage is bad for business, raises costs and so raises prices. Rossi, apparently, flunked ECON 101. The cornerstone of economics is that productivity increases create wealth. Where that wealth ends up is critical to an economy. If productivity increases are shared between labor and business, the economy grows. If not, the economy is damaged by either inflation or deflation. Trickle-down economics [the idea that profits should go to high-income individuals, who will eventually pass it on to the rest of the economy] is, by its nature, deflationary. Wages that are too high relative to value added are inflationary. Ideally these forces balance in the free market. But as libertarians are fond of pointing out, there is no such thing as a free market, never has been.

Business is the main offender in preventing a free labor market. Unions arose because of the inherent advantage that business has in setting wage scales. Unions and management can balance each other out over time and a certain amount of head knocking. But labor and management are more often than not in imbalance, wages growing more slowly with reference to productivity gains. Minimum wage is a measure by government to redress imbalance and so reduce the head knocking outcomes. That is its purpose, a sane government making sane choices about ameliorating the conflict between two natural enemies so that the conflict doesn't spill out into the streets with torches and pitchforks. When politicians are invested in having one or the other of the sides win, the intent of minimum wages as law is corrupted. It is not intended to create winners and losers, it is intended to maintain order.

The Tenth Amendment

So while Dino Rossi is intent on corrupting a system that has worked for 75 years to mediate the inherent conflict of labor and industry, the neophyte politician Joe Miller, and others of the current crazy crop of Tea Party candidates, is decrying it as unconstitutional. Miller is among the Tenth Amendment idiots, no clearer in vision and no more honest in intent than were the idiots who forced the Tenth's inclusion in the Bill of Rights in the first place. The Tenth is meaningless.

The Tenth Amendment endeavors, in club-blunt words, to limit the power of the federal government to what was written in 1791 including the Tenth itself, seemingly negating all the effort of enacting the additional amendments. Government, both federal and state, should have saved their time if a pustule in the stream of competence such as is the Tea Party can succeed in convincing the public that all law post to the Tenth is illegal and unconstitutional.

The Tenth Amendment is a joke and was seen so when adopted solely to mollify the South that feared emancipation [of slaves] even then. The Southern States sought to freeze the argument over slavery with the Tenth. They might have succeeded had it not been for the simple logic that the venerable document that formed the nation was left unfinished for sake of the expediency of placating the slavers. The Tenthers then seem to be arguing that a Constitution that denies the personhood of tens of percents of the population is just fine with them, even though the prime tenet of the Declaration is that all men are created equal, self evidently. Not so self evident to the King [of England] or to the Tea Party it seems.

The Tenth states, "The powers not delegated to the United States by the Constitution, nor prohibited by it to the States, are reserved to the States respectively, or to the people." It does not say that laws derived under and consistent with the Articles of the Constitution cannot be enacted over and above the original writing or that States, and certainly not individual citizens, obtain a power from it to overrule federal law or amendments duly adopted by two thirds of the states. The authority for making law over and above the words in the original Constitution is based in implied powers and is among the earliest arguments in Constitutional law. Implied powers are derived from the general welfare and necessary and proper clauses of the Preamble. Under the Tea Party interpretation that the Tenth limits the federal government in imposition of post ratification law, the Tenth is, logically, self nullifying. There can be no power to amend the Constitution that is asserted by a denial of its power to amend itself. It could just as easily be amended to say "we were just kidding with the Tenth". What defines law is a recognition of what best serves all or at least most of us, it is that we all agree on the enlightened and progressive thought that is the Preamble on which the Constitution and all law that follows is based. Anything that does not meet this measure is simply not sustainable as law.

No court in the land that has more than a trained ape in the seat of justice will uphold a challenge to Minimum Wage as it passes the test of promoting the general welfare. You would have to believe in Trickle Down economics to believe that it would not, and no one any longer believes in Trickle Down, if they ever did. Joe Miller is out on a Constitutional limb that won't support a down feather, and is an attorney. All you can conclude is that he is the most intellectually dishonest cracker to run for the Senate since "Tail Gunner" Joe McCarthy [a Republican senator from Wisconsin from 1947 to 1957 known for fueling fears of Communist subversion].

The War on Minimum Wage

In 1968 the Minimum Wage was $1.80 per hour. On that hourly wage, in 40 hours a week, you could support a family of four with a stay at home mom in most of the country. The CPI [Consumer Price Index, which measures the price level of consumer goods] has drifted around and the political climate has changed since then, and now the minimum wage will support about two thirds of one person. You have to double up in housing and transportation to get by on it now. Don't add children or you will need food stamps and Medicaid, things invented to fight wage deflation.

The reason Minimum Wage won't support a person is that Republicans have been winning their war on Minimum Wage and Democrats have been tepid to chilly in defending it. The moderate Democrats seem to have bought into the idea that a growing economy and a free markets obviate the need for it. In this they are wrong, but not as wrong as are Republicans.

The drift away from support for Minimum Wage has been ill advised on several levels.

There is no free market for wages without government support. Business and corporations exert incessant pressure to lower wages and benefits with massive advantages. Against that pressure the only recourse without government involvement is labor unions. The National Labor Relations Board [NLRB] was created to balance the playing field. Unions have been eviscerated starting with [President Ronald] Reagan's appointments to the NLRB of anti-union hard liners. Union busting became its own industry and wages have been in decline ever since. The fair market for labor, created by the New Deal Wagner Act [in 1935], was destroyed by Republican governments. Minimum wage, as an act of Congress, is now the main tool in balancing the benefits of economic growth, and without it, the economy is hostage to the willful misapprehensions of wage and economy dynamics of business and the Republicans.

Now, attacks on the minimum wage are the final resort of business to maintain profitability in markets put into decline by their own anti-labor agenda. Should they succeed in eliminating the minimum wage, there is no bottom for wages in America short of parity with the $2 a day scales of the third world. Business still fails to comprehend that a world filled with subsistence consumers will not power profits of any kind, not even with slaves as laborers.

It is an insanity of the gravest kind that business does not recognize the fate to which their aspirations lead. A world of impoverished people will not produce rich people. The already rich don't care. But those that follow, their own children and the working class of the world, should care, for they inherit the consequences of their parents and their parents employers' insatiable greed.

Assault on the minimum wage is not only an assault on the working class, it's an assault on the economy of the United States of America and all but an arrogant few whose futures do not depend on that economy. In the parlance of total warfare, it's the ultimate act of war. So, it's more than medicine for the greedy business boys and girls, it's really badly needed life saving medicine that they are marshaling armies of lobbyists and Tea Party zombies to resist. It's manifestly stupid to support them for not wanting to take the medicine.

Note

1. The Tea Party is a loose popular movement opposed to big government.

Periodical and Internet Sources Bibliography

The following articles have been selected to supplement the diverse views presented in this chapter.

Jared Bernstein	"Minimum Wage and Its Effects on Small Businesses," Economic Policy Institute, April 30, 2004. www.epi.org.
CNNMoney.com	"Wal-Mart Calls for Minimum Wage Hikes," October 25, 2005. http://money.cnn.com.
Christian Farr and BJ Lutz	"Wal-Mart Offers $8.75 Minimum Wage," NBC Chicago, June 21, 2010. www.nbcchicago.com.
Roger Koopman	"The Minimum Wage; Good Intentions, Bad Results," *Freeman*, March 1988.
Kris Maher	"Minimum-Wage Increase Comes at a Bad Time for Weakened Economy," *Wall Street Journal*, July 6, 2009.
Lori Montgomery	"Maverick Costco CEO Joins Push to Raise Minimum Wage," *Washington Post*, January 30, 2007.
MSNBC	"Economists Call for Minimum Wage to Be Raised," October 11, 2006. www.msnbc.msn.com.
Finn Orfano	"Does the Minimum Wage Law Stifle Small Business?," Bright Hub, October 29, 2009. www.brighthub .com.
Megan Poinski	"Supporters Say Hiking Minimum Wage Helps Economy, Opponents Say It Hurts," MarylandReporter. com, March 4, 2011. http://marylandreporter.com.
John Shelpley	"Business Owner Speaks at Press Conf. Launching Campaign to Raise Maryland Minimum Wage," Business for a Fair Minimum Wage, January 18, 2011. www. businessforafairminimumwage.org.

CHAPTER 3

How Does the Minimum Wage Affect Immigration?

Chapter Preface

In 2010, Karsten Lauritzen, the spokesman on immigration for the Danish ruling liberal party Venestre, stated that he wanted to exempt immigrants from Denmark's minimum wage. Instead of being paid a hundred kroner (around twenty US dollars) an hour, immigrants would receive only fifty kroner an hour. The lower wage would last about six months, Lauritzen suggested. "The high minimum wage is a barrier to get immigrants into work. So if we want to get the immigrants out of the ghettos we will have to pay less," he said, as quoted by Alex Rossi in a July 16, 2010, article on the Sky News website.

The proposal was cautiously supported by the Conservative Party spokesman Carena Christensen, who said, "It could definitely be a solution. We are open for good actions that can be done to bring the numbers down. The more that could be active in the work market, the better," as quoted in a February 6, 2011, article on the website Only in Denmark. Naser Kader, the immigration spokesman for the Conservatives, and an immigrant himself, also was open to the idea. Kader, however, specified that the lower rates should "only apply to immigrants arriving in the country without any Danish and whose training qualifications were not recognised," according to Tony Paterson writing in a July 19, 2010, article in London's *Independent* newspaper.

Despite the support from the Conservatives, Lauitzen's proposal was very controversial, even within his own party. Birthe Ronn Hornbech, Venestre's integration minister, said that the proposal was "disagreeable," and that it would stigmatize immigrants, as quoted by Anna Reimann in a July 15, 2010, article in the German magazine *Der Spiegel*. Left-wing parties also objected to the idea.

More surprisingly, the right-wing populist Danish People's Party (DF) opposed the idea. The DF is strongly anti-immigration, and so would not usually come out in favor of equal treatment for immigrants. In this case, however the party was worried that the lower wage would encourage employers to hire immigrants. As a result, the party concluded, nonimmigrant workers "would . . . find it harder to find work if [the law] were implemented," according to *Der Spiegel*.

The following viewpoints address issues around immigration and the minimum wage in the United States.

"By raising the federal minimum wage, and strengthening its enforcement, Congress would take the profit out of hiring illegal immigrants."

Raising and Enforcing the Minimum Wage Would Reduce Illegal Immigration

Ivan Light

Ivan Light is professor of sociology at the University of California, Los Angeles and the author of Deflecting Immigration: Networks, Markets, and Regulation in Los Angeles. *In the following viewpoint he argues that securing the border will not have much impact on illegal immigration. Instead, he says, illegal immigration should be discouraged by raising the minimum wage and by enforcing safety and workplace standards. He says that better wages and working conditions will make it uneconomical for businesses to hire illegal immigrants. Without jobs for immigrants, he concludes, illegal immigration will be drastically reduced.*

As you read, consider the following questions:

1. According to Light, why do Republicans not call for a wall across the entire Mexican border?

2. How did California deflect 2 million Mexican immigrants to other states, according to the author?

3. In Light's view, why do many politicians not want to take effective action to stem immigration?

Illegal immigration into the United States is a problem that needs solution. A product of globalization, illegal immigration is worldwide, and does not trouble only the United States. Europe has its own problems with illegal immigration. For example, France has 400,000 illegal immigrants who represent about 5% of their immigrant population. Yes, the USA's problem of illegal immigration is worse than Europe's, partially because of geography, but we have also ignored the problem for 20 years then abruptly rediscovered it. Panic-driven hysteria about illegal immigration will succeed in wasting taxpayer money, but will fail to solve the problem. We need to devote serious, concerted attention to solving this problem in a cost-effective way that minimizes damage to our friendly relationship with Mexico and to our international reputation for equal accessibility by immigrants of all cultures and races. This is possible.

Not a Mortal Danger

House Republicans have declared that illegal migration poses a "mortal danger" to the United States. Yes, illegal immigration is a problem, but does it pose a mortal danger? Consider this. If the population of the United States contained the same density of immigrants that the population of California already contains, then the United States could absorb the entire population of Mexico, about 90 million additional people. Clearly immigrants are a problem for California, but the Golden State has not collapsed under their weight, and neither would the United States even under this worst-case scenario. A problem, yes, but illegal immigration does not pose a mortal danger to the United States.

House Republicans have recommended that the United States build a wall along the Mexico/US border. But read the fine print. Supporters want to build a wall along only 750 miles of the 2,000 mile border with Mexico. If stretched along the entire border, the Great Wall of America would be impossibly expensive to build and monitor so the Republicans have asked for only a 750-mile wall. Unfortunately, illegal immigrants will go around a short wall just as the Germans went around the Maginot line in 1940 [when the French put up a line of fortifications to stop German invasion]. A short wall will slightly slow the illegal immigration but it will do nothing to cause the repatriation of illegal immigrants already here.

Don't we need that wall to keep out terrorists? No, a wall is not a cost-effective solution to terrorist infiltration. First of all, the United States has 10,000 miles of seacoast border to patrol (including Puerto Rico). Terrorists won't be stopped by militarization of the entire Mexican border, much less a 750-mile wall. Second, of the 9-11 perpetrators, none entered the United States by sneaking across our borders without inspection. All entered the United States legally, and some were still in the United States legally when they committed their heinous crimes. Most had become visa abusers who entered the United States legally, then overstayed and melted into the general population. A wall will do nothing to stop terrorists who enter the United States legally then overstay their visa. The cost-effective way to stop terrorists is to monitor islamicist cells as the British police have successfully done. To protect ourselves against terrorists, we should improve our cooperation with the British police, learn from their methods, and strengthen ties with police forces of other friendly countries.

Worse, even if that immigration wall were full-length, and even if it stopped 100% of those who seek to enter the United States without inspection, the wall would only stop 60% of illegal immigrants. That is because 40% of illegal immigrants enter the United States legally, then overstay their visas, and melt into the

California, Immigrants, and the Minimum Wage

The worsening economic situation among Latinos came to be perceived as a social problem. To remedy it, multiethnic social movements mobilized to combat low wages among immigrants. Raising the minimum wage was a favored approach. In 1987, three Los Angeles affiliates of the Industrial Areas Foundation undertook a successful campaign to raise California's minimum wage to $4.25 an hour, the highest in the nation. They succeeded—putting California's minimum wage at 105 percent of the federal, up from 102 percent in the 1970s. During the 1960s and 1950s, California's minimum wage had coincided with Washington's. However, after this 1987 increase, California continued to set its minimum wage higher than the federal, reaching 112 percent in 2000. The state's high minimum wage discouraged low-wage firms from remaining in Caifornia, and thus helped to deflect the low-wage workers who would otherwise have held jobs in those firms.

Ivan Light, Deflecting Immigration:
Networks, Markets, and Regulations in
Los Angeles, *2006.*

general population. Once they overstay their visa, legal visitors become illegal immigrants. A full-length wall would do nothing to stop this 40% of visa abusers, nor will it induce any illegal immigrants already here to return to their homelands.

Possibly we should deport all the illegal immigrants already here? Yes, indeed, if we can catch them, we should deport them, but illegal immigrants are hard to catch. You cannot deport people you cannot catch. Moreover, there are already between eight and thirteen million illegal immigrants in the U.S. If the federal government could apprehend, try, and deport all these illegals at a cost of $1,000 each, a modest estimate, it would cost the taxpayers $13 trillion dollars [sic] to deport the entire illegal population. That is 40 times more than the war in Iraq has already cost. We need to induce illegal immigrants to repatriate at their own expense, not the taxpayer's.

A Policy of Attrition

Happily, a policy of immigration reduction by attrition offers a realistic, cost-effective way to curb new illegal immigrants and to induce some of those already here to repatriate at their own expense. A policy of attrition reduces illegal immigration by reducing the access of illegal immigrants to jobs and housing in this country. By checking Social Security numbers, a single clerk in Washington, D.C. can keep out more illegal immigrants than a thousand soldiers on the Mexican border. At a minimum, this clerk needs to advise employers whenever employees have bogus Social Security numbers. When so notified, employers must discharge those employees. No such legal arrangement currently exists! All it takes to create it is an act of Congress. At that point, the federal government could mount a reliable prosecution of scoff-law employers. This plan would shut down the job supply for illegal immigrants, discouraging additional migration, and also would compel unemployed illegal immigrants already here to return to their homeland at their own expense, not at the expense of the U.S. taxpayer.

There are additional cost-effective measures that will restrict illegal immigration by attrition without antagonizing Mexico. By raising the federal minimum wage, and strengthening its enforcement, Congress would take the profit out of hiring illegal immigrants. Illegal immigrants are not profitable to employ at high wages. This is a proven remedy. By raising its minimum wage 12% above the federal level, California deflected two million Mexican immigrants to other states. Facing a higher minimum wage, firms dependent upon cheap immigrant labor would close, and illegal immigrants would lose their jobs.

Still not enough? By enforcing existing occupational, safety, and health legislation, Congress would additionally take the profit out of cheap-labor sweatshops, causing employers of the cheapest labor to fire existing illegal workers without replacing them. Illegal immigrants are not profitable if employers must provide safe and sanitary working conditions. If safe and sanitary conditions must be provided, employers will hire native-born workers. Still not enough? By enforcing existing housing legislation Congress (supported by 50 state governments) can shut down the slums in which illegal immigrants live. Because their wages are pitifully low, illegal immigrants mainly live in slums so shutting down slums deprives them of affordable housing. Unable to find low-wage work or to live in slums, illegal immigrants would be compelled to repatriate at their own expense. Moreover, many fewer will come from staging areas south of the border. The Center for Migration Studies estimates that within five years a federal policy of attrition could reduce the existing population of illegal immigrants in the United States by one half. The cost would be modest.

Better Understanding Is Needed

If illegal immigration can so cheaply be reduced, then why has it not already been done? Two big problems exist. The first is a lack of public understanding of the elementary facts about immigration. This misunderstanding leads the uninformed to suppose that the only way to stop illegal immigration is to "regain control of the border." This idea translates into strengthening borders with walls, inspections, soldiers and mine fields. The Congressional Budget Office estimates that the Senate's "secure borders" reform would, if fully enacted, "reduce the net flow of illegal immigrants by one-quarter" and will cost 22.7 billion dollars between 2008 and 2017.

Evidently, militarizing borders will only slightly reduce illegal immigration and it will cost a great deal of money. It will also antagonize Mexico. They booed our Miss Universe contestant in Mexico City in May 2007, and a militarized border will worsen our relationship with Mexico. Alas, a cost-effective, non-antagonistic policy of attrition is not on the political agenda of either party because neither the politicians nor the general public understands the problem.

Second, many important politicians really do not want to take effective action to stem illegal immigration. Understanding that border enforcement will fail, they nonetheless offer border enforcement to the public. A failing policy fits their political agenda, while a border enforcement potlatch gets them reelected. The dominant Wall Street wing of the Republican Party wants open borders. The Wall Street wing of the Republican Party frankly encourages and supports illegal immigration. Representing this wing, President [George W.] Bush backed the "Secure Borders, Economic Opportunity, and Immigration Reform Act of 2007." As its name implies, this bi-partisan Senate legislation emphasized border enforcement. The leadership of the Democratic Party also backed this bill but for a different reason. The leadership of the Democratic Party is afraid to antagonize Hispanic voters, on whom the party's long-term electoral prospects are thought to depend. Therefore, the Democratic leadership joined President Bush and the Wall Street Republicans in support of the Senate immigration reform. This bill was defeated on June 7, 2007 by a combination of amnesty-hating Republicans and trade union/labor rights Democrats.

Cost-Effective Solutions

When the Senate bill comes back, as Senator Harry Reid, the majority leader, has promised it will, the shotgun reform will contain one cost-effective provision amid a host of cost-ineffective provisions directed at border security. The cost-effective provision is federal surveillance of social security numbers to detect unauthorized workers anywhere in the 50 states. Of the 10 billion dollars that the Congressional Budget Office expects this immigration reform to cost between 2008 and 2012, an estimated 12% will be devoted to surveillance of social security numbers. What if, having militarized the border, we later learn that 90% of the beneficial effect of this legislation was accomplished by 12% of the money appropriated? This possibility could have been tested in advance by funding the social security legislation alone in 2008, and waiting until 2010 to ascertain the consequences. If surveillance of social security numbers proves effective, as it very well might, then militarization of the borders would not be needed at all, and the federal government would have saved 9 billion dollars as well as our friendly relationship with Mexico.

Conclusion: Do not militarize the borders at great expense until more cost-effective solutions have been tried.

"An increase in the minimum wage will actually open up more jobs for illegal immigrants."

Raising the Minimum Wage Would Not Reduce Illegal Immigration

David R. Henderson

David R. Henderson is a research fellow with the Hoover Institution and an economics professor at the Naval Postgraduate School. In the following viewpoint he argues that raising the minimum wage will not discourage illegal immigration. Raising the minimum wage, he contends, will not cause more Americans to take low-wage jobs; it will just cause those jobs to disappear. Even if the jobs do not disappear, Henderson maintains, there will actually be even more incentive to give such jobs to illegal immigrants because illegal immigrants paid less than minimum wage are afraid to go to the authorities.

As you read, consider the following questions:

1. Who are Dukakis and Mitchell, according to Henderson?
2. How many full-time workers does the author estimate

were engaged in enforcing wage regulations in 2005?

3. According to Henderson, the main enforcement of minimum wage is initiated by whom?

In "Raise Wages, Not Walls," an op-ed in the July 25 [2006] *New York Times*, Michael Dukakis and Daniel Mitchell make a proposal that is breathtaking in its misunderstanding of basic economics. After showing problems with the various congressional proposals to limit illegal immigration, they give their own solution: increase the minimum wage. They write, "If we are really serious about turning back the tide of illegal immigration, we should start by raising the minimum wage from $5.15 per hour to something closer to $8." This, they argue, will make currently low-wage jobs more attractive to people who are legally in the United States. Making Americans more willing to work at these jobs, they write, would deny "them [the jobs] to people who aren't supposed to be here in the first place." They don't specify how this would deny jobs to illegal immigrants, but seem to place their faith in "tough enforcement of wage rules."

Misunderstanding Economics

But here's the irony. The proposal would reduce the number of jobs available to people here legally and give illegal immigrants an advantage in the competition for jobs. Dukakis and Mitchell reach a mistaken conclusion by confusing demand and supply, and showing a misunderstanding of how the minimum wage is enforced. That Dukakis, a former presidential candidate and a political science professor at Northeastern University, made such a mistake in economic reasoning is understandable. That Mitchell, a professor of management and public policy at UCLA, did so is less understandable: both his B.A. (Columbia) and his Ph.D. (MIT) are in economics.

When the minimum wage rises, what happens? Some jobs that were worth hiring someone to do are no longer worth filling. The jobs lost are the most marginal ones, the ones that had low value and that paid little. That's why the vast majority of studies of the minimum wage have found that increases, all other things [being] equal, reduce the number of low-skilled jobs offered and filled.

Surely Dukakis, a public-policy wonk for the whole of his adult life, and Mitchell, a trained economist, must know that. So how do Dukakis and Mitchell contend with that fact? First, they admit it—kind of. They write, "If we raise the minimum wage, it's possible some low-end jobs may be lost." Notice the redundancy in "it's possible" and "may." A good editor, and I'm sure the *New York Times* has many, would have caught this and said: "'It's possible' means the same thing as 'may' and so you should drop one." Why didn't an editor do this? My guess is that the editor, like Dukakis and Mitchell, wanted to create the idea that the job loss would be small. By hedging twice, the authors leave that impression in many readers' minds.

But still, there's job loss, and even they, in their "just maybe" way, admit it. So how do they get to the conclusion that a higher minimum wage would help Americans? They write that if the government increased the minimum wage, "more Americans would also be willing to work in such [previously low-paying] jobs." That's true. When the minimum wage goes up, jobs that wouldn't have been attractive to some people will be attractive to them. But the objection to the minimum wage has never been about whether more people would be willing to work at a higher wage than would be willing to work at a lower wage. The problem is that being willing to work at a job isn't enough: someone has to be willing to offer you that job. If simple willingness to work were enough to get you a job, then a classic "Seinfeld" episode wouldn't have been funny. In that episode George Costanza is out of work and wants a job. He sits around with Jerry Seinfeld trying to decide what kind of job he should get. George comes up with the idea of being a sports commentator and lays out how much fun that would be. The audience laughs because they realize that George's simple willingness to work is not enough:

another necessary condition is that someone think he's good enough to be worth the high pay that sports commentators get. I bet even Dukakis and Mitchell, if they saw that episode, would laugh. Which is why they should laugh at their own proposal—if not for its tragic consequences.

Misunderstanding Enforcement

But wait a minute, Dukakis and Mitchell might say: there's still a thin spot of light at the end of our constructed tunnel. They argue that raising the minimum wage and increasing its enforcement will push illegal immigrants out of jobs and make these jobs available for Americans. It is true that if the minimum wage caused the number of illegal immigrants working to fall more than the total number of jobs fell, there would be more minimum-wage jobs for Americans. But is this likely? No, and in thinking it likely, they show a misunderstanding of how the minimum wage is enforced.

Their model of enforcement, it seems, is of diligent federal workers going into workplaces and checking records on wages paid. But employers willing to break the law on wages are likely to be willing to break the law on record-keeping. In 2005 the U.S. Department of Labor's Wage and Hour Division put 969,776 hours into enforcement of all parts of the federal wage regulations. This would translate into only 500 full-time workers nationwide. And not all of these were involved in enforcing the minimum wage: some were enforcing overtime regulations, child-labor regulations, and more. So even quadrupling the number of enforcers would not make a major dent when the number of low-wage employers would likely be in the hundreds of thousands.

The main enforcement of the minimum wage is initiated by employees, not by the government. An employee who thinks he was paid less than the minimum can contact the federal government or the state labor board and show his pay records. Then the government collects back wages and a fine from the employer. In 2005 the Labor Department reported 30,375 complaints registered about employer violations of wage and hours laws. The vast majority of these complaints were likely by employees. That's why the minimum wage is so effective. But employers aren't typically stupid. They know this risk, which is why even employers who have no ethical qualms about breaking the law hesitate to hire people at less than the minimum wage.

Immigrants Do Not Complain

But there's one type of employee that the employer is not so afraid of hiring and paying less than the minimum: an illegal immigrant. Illegal immigrants are nervous about going to the government to report that they were paid less than the minimum. Employers, knowing this, are more willing to hire them. So while reducing the overall number of jobs, an increase in the minimum wage will actually open up more jobs for illegal immigrants, making it even harder for unskilled legal residents to find work.

How can not being able to sic the government on an employer be an advantage? However much someone might plead with an employer to offer him a job at below minimum wage, if the employer knows the employee can sue for back wages, he probably won't offer the job. But not being able to sue because the job candidate is here illegally makes his promise not to sue credible, which also means he doesn't even need to make such a promise. The illegal immigrant gets the job.

*"If the minimum wage law were
repealed, U.S. employers could begin
hiring U.S. residents . . . to complete
the jobs that the illegal immigrants
previously handled."*

Abolishing the Minimum Wage Would Reduce Illegal Immigration

Economic Edge

Economic Edge is a website devoted to economic advice and analysis. The following viewpoint argues that the minimum wage causes illegal immigration. The minimum wage creates a black market for labor worth less than minimum wage, the viewpoint contends. It argues that getting rid of the minimum wage would mean that US citizens could be hired to do the jobs illegal immigrants do now. With the incentive to immigrate removed, the author concludes, illegal immigration would stop, and the labor market would function normally.

As you read, consider the following questions:

1. What does Economic Edge say will happen if minimum wage is set at six dollars an hour to those whose work is

worth less than that?

2. According to the author, what kind of mentality does the minimum wage enforce?

3. What will ensure that workers are paid a fair wage, according to Economic Edge?

L ately, there's been a lot of talk about strengthening the southern border between the U.S. and Mexico to prevent the continued mass influx of illegal immigrants. Proponents of "open borders" claim that

1. Immigrants perform work that Americans don't want to perform (such as manual labor, agricultural work, janitorial services, etc.). This is not a very valid argument, in my opinion.

2. Immigrants help keep the price of goods lower. Since the employer is not required to pay minimum wage, he can pass on this "cost savings" to the consumer, in the form of lower prices.

Minimum Wage and the Black Market

The main attraction for immigrants is a better standard of living for themselves and their families in the U.S. (achieved as a result of higher wages). We would not have an "illegal immigration problem" if U.S. employers refused to hire illegal immigrants. So, at first glance, the problem appears to be employers—employers who are ignoring the rules against hiring illegal immigrants.

But the more important question is "Why are U.S. employers circumventing (or deliberately ignoring) the laws that restrict hiring illegal workers?"

Answer: The root cause of illegal Mexican immigration is the mandatory minimum wage law. The minimum wage law forces employers to pay more than "fair market value" for wages.

"HELP WANTED: Jobs, Jobs, Jobs; Almost Minimum wage!," cartoon by Ed Fischer, www .CartoonStock.com. Copyright © Ed Fischer. Reproduction rights obtainable from www .CartoonStock.com.

If an employer has to pay more than "fair market value" for wages, then he is less competitive in the marketplace, and he is forced to charge higher prices to his customers (to compensate for the increased cost of labor). Increased cost of labor sharply cuts into business revenue. It is difficult to turn a profit when the government enacts legislation mandating what you can pay for labor . . . especially when the marketplace of laborers is willing to work for less than the mandated minimum wage.

The minimum wage law puts forced price controls on the economy, so that a black market develops to circumvent that forced control (similar to prohibition laws in the 1920's [that outlawed alcohol]). Basically, the minimum wage law unfairly manipulates supply and demand and creates an artificial price floor. A "fair wage" is the intersection of supply and demand. The minimum wage law *ignores supply and demand* and attempts to regulate the economy by forced mandate. Which, of course, fails miserably, and leads to an illegal "black market" for immigrants who will work for less.

There are countless other economic problems created by the federal minimum wage law; one of the biggest is a higher rate of unemployment. Countries with minimum wage laws have higher unemployment rates than countries without such laws.

This can be seen with the following example: If the minimum wage is $6/hour, then an employer will only offer somone a job when the value of his work exceeds $6/hour. So, only people whose value to a company exceeds $6/hour will find employment. All others will face unemployment (or the option to work illegally for less).

Additionally, the minimum wage law reinforces dependence and an "entitlement" mentality. Many new workers (i.e. teenagers) and unskilled laborers feel they are "entitled" to a certain amount regardless of the value they provide to a company, and regardless of prevailing market conditions (supply and demand). This has disastrous social implications and further reinforces the "welfare state" mentality.

Many argue that without minimum wage laws, workers would be exploited and could not maintain a decent standard of living. However, this is not true. As Mark Tier points out in his article "Jobs for Everyone," "[In] any labor market where there are no restrictions on the employment of labor, employees know their own worth, their market value, and if you don't pay them what they are worth, they'll quickly find someone who will." The free market will make sure that workers are paid a fair wage that is commensurate with their skills, abilities, and the value they provide to a company.

How to Be Rid of Illegal Immigration

Stationing more federal troops at the Mexican border will not solve the illegal immigration problem. Determined immigrants will find a way to sneak past border patrols. The only way to permanently solve the problem is to eliminate the root cause—no jobs for illegals means no massive influx of illegals.

Threatening U.S. employers with fines/lawsuits and imposing additional regulation (and monitoring) of the workers they hire will not solve the problem. *The government must create a financial incentive for U.S. employers to refuse to hire illegal immigrants.* The best way to do so is to repeal the federal minimum wage law.

If the minimum wage law were repealed, U.S. employers could begin hiring U.S. residents (many of whom are on unemployment) to complete the jobs that the illegal immigrants previously handled. Once this is done, supply and demand will resolve the border problem naturally.

Less supply of jobs for illlegals equals less demand (desire) to cross the U.S. border.

| "*The minimum wage issue doesn't affect illegal immigrants.*"

The Minimum Wage Is Irrelevant to Illegal Immigration

Thomas Andrew Olson

Thomas Andrew Olson is a writer and speaker. In the following viewpoint he argues that raising the minimum wage does little to address unemployment or to move people out of poverty. He adds that raising wages would not increase the hiring of native workers to replace illegal immigration. Instead, he says, to ensure significantly higher wages would require serious government intervention and would result in hardship for employers, consumers, and workers. He concludes that calls for increases in the minimum-wage and for reduction of illegal immigration are largely political posturing.

As you read, consider the following questions:

1. What percentage of workers does Olson say received the minimum wage in 2002?
2. What wage can undocumented lettuce pickers in California earn, according to the author?

3. According to Dobbs, as cited by Olson, why would it be difficult to fix prices of vegetables in the United States?

CNN anchor Lou Dobbs' major raison d'être these days is the issue of "illegal" immigration, as well as that of self-appointed champion of America's shrinking middle class. While I may not support every one of his opinions (and indeed, I have a few of my own on immigration), I will give him credit for placing such issues—and the government's lame response—squarely in the face of the public. He has grown a very focused and loyal viewer base, and from the sound of their comments, they intend to be a thorn in the sides of their elected representatives this year [2006]. That is always a good thing, and again, I'll give Dobbs the props he deserves for getting voters mobilized.

Minimum Wage and Economic Issues

But there are some places where I feel he glosses over a topic in exchange for a good sound bite. The two cases in point regard his views on a proposed minimum wage increase and the overall economics of illegal immigration.

In a recent op-ed, Dobbs claimed that an increase of the minimum wage to $7.15 an hour is long overdue, will help bring people out of poverty, and will not hurt overall unemployment statistics:

> The myth that raising the minimum wage will lead to job cuts is just that: a myth. In fact, research suggests just the opposite. According to the Fiscal Policy Institute, since 1998, states with higher minimum wages experienced better job growth than states paying only the federal minimum wage. Among small retail businesses in those higher minimum-wage states, job growth was double the rest of the country.

What does one have to do with the other?? The vast majority of jobs in this country already pay more than the minimum wage. We need to look at the general economic picture of those states before we jump to any conclusions. What kind of jobs are they talking about, and who is doing them? A hot local job market will demand higher wages across the board, regardless of what the mandated minimum wages are.

Here are some other pesky facts that Dobbs failed to mention in his op-ed:

- According to the Bureau of Labor Statistics 2002 report, of the 72.7 million hourly-wage workers in the US, only 2.2 million, a mere 3%, received minimum wages. While that's bad for them, it's not a national crisis.
- Only 5.3% of minimum-wage workers come from families below the poverty line.
- The highest proportion of minimum wage workers were in the retail trade (8%), whereas agriculture only claimed *2%*.
- The vast majority of minimum wage workers either have second jobs or live with other family members and are not sole-source providers of income.
- Minimum wages provide artificial barriers to those seeking their first job experience. Unemployment among 16–19-year-olds was 17.3% in 2005, as opposed to 5.6% overall. When split out by ethnicity, Hispanic and black teens had unemployment rates of *25% and 40%* respectively. Analysts have been railing for decades about the social effects of youth unemployment, without even considering as a potential causative factor the ever-increasing minimum wage during all that time.

While the idea of raising minimum wages may provide a feel-good sound bite, it does nothing to address economic issues in specific sectors of our population that are affected most by unemployment. A productive employee won't be getting minimum wage for long, as it's in the employer's best interest to retain productive talent, and they know they have to pay more for it or lose it to the competition. And, as many have argued at

Mises.org, Cato, and elsewhere, if minimum wages were an economic panacea, why stop at $7.15? Why not $12, $20, or $100?

Illegal Immigrants Unaffected

It also appears that the minimum wage issue doesn't affect illegal immigrants, either.

"Amnesty" proponents [who want illegal immigrants to be granted citizenship] often proclaim that the so-called "undocumenteds" do work that American citizens either (a) won't do, period, or (b) won't do for the kind of wages and benefits offered by employers, particularly when it comes to harvesting produce.

Again, according to Lou Dobbs, "undocumented" lettuce pickers in California earn an average of $9 an hour. This is significantly *higher* than the minimum wage, however, which suggests there is actual *competition* for those jobs even among so-called undocumenteds. Nevertheless, the message is that US citizens fail to show up, and there is an abundance of illegals willing to work. So the farmers do what they have to in order to get the crop in—nudge-nudge-wink-wink—and of course conveniently save a lot of money in wages and benefits while they're at it.

But what Dobbs recommends as a remedy is something out of [German socialist philosopher Friedrich] Engels. He claimed that if growers raised the price of a head of lettuce by *only ten cents*, they could afford to pay the harvesters Dobbs' idea of a "living wage" of $16 per hour. This sea change, combined with tough enforcement of laws banning the hiring of illegals, would somehow attract heretofore recalcitrant US workers. Seeing the opportunities dry up in the face of newly inspired domestic competition, the undocumented Mexicans would drift back over the border of their own accord, and that would be that.

Hurting Workers and Consumers

There are several problems with this idea:

• In the first place, I can see them trying to jack up the price a dime a head and even forcing employers to pay more—but they'll never combine that with strict enforcement of labor laws, which would leave the US more attractive to undocumented workers than ever. Think it's bad now? Try doubling the wages and watch the Mexican flood come in.

• According to [grocery chain] Safeway, the price this week for a head of iceberg lettuce is $1.49. So raising it a dime makes it 1.59. If you eat two heads a week, that's a $10.40/annum increase. Now multiply that times all the *other* fruits and veggies you and your family would like to consume in a year—it adds up quickly. If you are at the low end of the economic scale, the pinch is even tighter, and you may end up being unable to purchase all the nourishing food you require, settling for either reduced quality, or alternatives that aren't as nutritious, which could impact your long term health.

• The last time I checked, there wasn't a veggie-grower *cartel* in this country, involved in uniform price-fixing. Perhaps if there were, Dobbs' plan could be carried out via some sort of egregious federal legislation—and you could count on the Congress to do it, if it would placate enough voters. There are still—albeit subsidized—independent growers of produce in this country, who remain at least nominally in competition. Even if some growers were convinced to raise their prices and pay their workers more, they would be under increased economic pressure and risk losing significant market share, as others would not see the need for change. Ergo, unless everyone agreed, or were forced to by law, it simply will not happen.

• If such a plan was legislated by Congress, we would all pay a high price for it. The agricultural lobby is powerful, their clients having received subsidies for seven decades or longer. You can bet such a bill wouldn't be passed unless those subsidies were increased, as well. Of course, as it costs the government thirty cents or so to deliver every dime's worth of "benefit", the increased costs to taxpayers for that "living wage" head of lettuce could really add up.

• But wait, the nightmare isn't over. Now we have lettuce growers being forced by government fiat (and increased subsidies) to pay $16/hr and "hire American". Where will they find the workers they need if they can't hire illegals? I can visualize this flood of unemployed youth from South Central L.A. spreading out into the central California countryside and trying to harvest vegetables for the first time in their lives. A sudden, dramatic increase in wages might indeed attract more homegrown workers, but are they the workers the farmers need? Will they actually bring some coordination and a good work ethic to the job? Presumably not. So the farmers, despite their subsidies, now have to contend with a bunch of overpriced, inexperienced, attitude-challenged workers to bring in their crops. Expect reduced productivity and a lot more waste—and I would also expect the cost of a head of lettuce to go up a lot higher than a dime. Say what you will about "living wages", but those new-hire's skills would not be worth $16/hr. They're probably not worth $9. It will be an economic disaster for all involved, and the growers (and their customers) will be pining for the "illegal" Mexicans to return and restore stability.

One could not pass legislation enforcing this without violating the rights of farmers, farm workers, taxpayers, and Americans of more modest means who can't afford higher grocery bills.

The minimum wage pseudo-debate is a typical election-year red herring, and Lou Dobbs should have known better than to fall for it. Our present immigration situation is the price Americans are willing to accept, whether they'll admit it or not, to have low-cost, plentiful and nourishing food on their tables, not to mention a lot of other services they don't want to pay a king's ransom to obtain. Dobbs' economic notions in both these debates are simply unsupported by political and economic reality, and would engender a social and economic nightmare to implement, but with no discernible long-term benefit.

| "Increasing the minimum wage and keeping unskilled immigration high may make the unemployment problem even worse."

Reducing Immigration Is Better Than Raising the Minimum Wage

Steven A. Camarota

Stephen A. Camarota is the director of research at the Center for Immigration Studies. In the following viewpoint, he argues that high levels of illegal immigration hurt poor, low-skilled native workers. He says that increasing the minimum wage to help poor workers has the danger of increasing unemployment further. On the other hand, he argues, reducing immigration through tougher enforcement could be an effective policy with fewer downsides.

As you read, consider the following questions:

1. How does the Earned Income Tax Credit act as a subsidy to employers, and why can that be a problem, according to Camarota?

2. What does the author say was the reason for the decline of

the illegal immigrant population in the United States from
2007 to 2009?

3. What does Camarota say the policy should be if the
United States places a high priority on helping the poor in
other countries?

Knowing that less-educated natives are made worse off by immigration does not tell us what, if anything, we should do
about it. The extent to which we take action to deal with the wage
and employment effects of immigration depends on how concerned we are about the wages of less-educated natives. A number
of scholars have argued that the inability of less-educated workers to find work and earn a living wage contributes significantly
to such social problems as welfare dependency, family breakup,
and crime. One need not accept all the arguments made in this
regard to acknowledge that a significant reduction in employment opportunities for the poorest Americans is a cause for real
concern.

Policy Options

Help Workers, but Leave Immigration Policy Unchanged. If
we wish to do something about the effects of immigration, there
are two possible sets of policy options that could be pursued. The
first set would involve leaving immigration policy in place and
doing more to ameliorate the harmful effects of immigration
on natives in lower-skilled occupations. Since the research indicates that the negative impact from immigration falls on those
employed at the bottom of the labor market, an increase in the
minimum wage may be helpful in offsetting some of the wage
effects of immigration, though doing so may exacerbate the unemployment effect. Most economists think that the minimum
wage tends to increase unemployment. Increasing the minimum
wage and keeping unskilled immigration high may make the unemployment problem even worse.

Another program that might be helpful in assisting those harmed by immigrant competition is the Earned Income Tax Credit (EITC), which provides cash to workers who pay no federal income tax. There is little doubt that the cash payments from the credit increase the income of low-wage workers. However, in addition to the high cost to taxpayers, the credit may also hold down wages because it acts as a subsidy to low-wage employers. That is, employers have less incentive to increase wages because workers are now being paid in part by the federal government. Cutting low and unskilled immigration, on the other hand, has no such downside for less-skilled workers, nor is it costly to taxpayers. Moreover, the credit only increases earnings for those with jobs, it does not address increased unemployment among the less-skilled that comes with immigration. Finally, it is not clear how much increasing the minimum wage or the EITC would be helpful in dealing with the decline in labor-force participation among less-educated natives. . . .

Reducing Unskilled Legal Immigration. The second set of policy options that might be enacted to deal with this problem would involve changing immigration policy with the intent of reducing job competition for natives and immigrants already here. If we were to reduce the immigration of less-educated immigrants we might want to change the selection criteria to ensure that immigrants entering the country will not compete directly with the poorest and most vulnerable workers. At present, only about 12 percent of legal immigrants are admitted based on their skills or education. Since two-thirds of permanent residency visas are issued based on family relationships, reducing the flow of less-educated legal immigrants would involve reducing the number of visas based on family relationships. This might include eliminating the preferences now in the law for the siblings and adult children (over 21) of U.S. citizens and the adult children of legal permanent residents. These changes would not only reduce the immigration of less-educated legal immigrants immediately, they would also limit the chain migration of less-educated immigrants that occurs as the spouses of those admitted in the sibling and adult child categories petition to bring in their relatives. The H-2B program, which allows workers into the country for seasonal non-agricultural work would also need to be eliminated.

Enforcement

Reducing Unskilled Illegal Immigration. In addition to reducing the flow of less-educated legal immigrants, a greater allocation of resources could be devoted to controlling illegal immigration, especially in the interior of the country. About half of the immigrants working in such occupations as construction, building cleaning and maintenance, and food processing and preparation are estimated to be illegal aliens according to my own analysis and research done by the Pew Hispanic Center. A strategy of attrition through enforcement offers the best hope of reducing illegal immigration. The goal of such a policy would be to make illegals go home or self deport. The former INS [Immigration and Naturalization Service] estimated that more than a quarter of million illegals went home on their own, were deported, or died each year. A recent study by the Center for Immigration Studies finds very strong evidence that illegal population has fallen from the first part of 2007 to the first part of 2009. Part of the reason for this decline was a substantial increase in illegal immigrants leaving the country.

The centerpiece to interior enforcement would be to enforce the law barring illegals from holding jobs by using national databases that already exist to ensure that each new hire is legally entitled to work here. The E-verify program with is currently voluntary for employers could be used in this regard. The IRS [Internal Revenue Service] must also stop accepting Social Security numbers that it knows are bogus. We also need to make a much greater effort to deny illegal aliens things like driver's licenses, bank accounts, loans, in-state college tuition, etc. Local

Employment of All Persons and Native-Born US Citizens, Second Quarter 2010

The table shows high rates of unemployment in 2010 among both native-born Americans and all persons in the US. Unemployment rates are especially high among young people and those without high school diplomas.

	Employed	Unemployed	Percent Unemployed		Not in Labor Force (18–65)	Employed	Total	Employment Rate
All Natives (16+)	**117,400**	**12,510**	**9.6%**	**All Natives (18–65)**	**39,011**	**111,360**	**161,992**	**68.7%**
Teens (16–17)	1,356	616	31.2%	Teens (16–17)	6,343	1,356	8,315	16.3%
<HS [high school] (18+)	6,751	1,774	20.8%	<HS (18–65)	7,265	6,324	15,331	41.2%
HS Only (18+)	33,783	4,747	12.3%	HS Only (18–65)	12,985	32,265	49,899	64.7%
HS Only (18–29)	7,670	1,922	20.0%	HS Only (18–29)	3,238	7,670	12,830	59.8%
Some College (18+)	36,415	3,535	8.8%	Some College (18–65)	12,061	35,315	50,843	69.5%
Bachelor's or More (18+)	39,095	1,839	4.5%	Bachelor's or More (18–65)	6,700	37,456	45,919	81.6%

	Employed	Unemployed	Percent Unemployed	All Persons (18–65)	Not in Labor Force (18–65)	Employed	Total	Employment Rate
All Persons (16+)	139,561	14,621	9.5%	All Persons (18–65)	46,199	132,861	192,711	68.9%
Teens (16–17)	1,421	654	31.5%	Teens (16–17)	6,817	1,421	8,892	16.0%
<HS (18+)	12,707	2,501	16.4%	<HS (18–65)	9,876	12,140	24,473	49.6%
HS Only (18+)	39,245	5,323	11.9%	HS Only (18–65)	14,788	37,591	57,589	65.3%
HS Only (18–29)	8,804	2,081	19.1%	HS Only (18–29)	3,653	8,804	14,538	60.6%
Some College (18+)	40,307	3,916	8.9%	Some College (18–65)	13,229	39,116	56,187	69.6%
Bachelor's or More (18+)	45,881	2,227	4.6%	Bachelor's or More (18–65)	8,306	44,014	54,462	80.8%

TAKEN FROM: Steven A. Camarota, "From Bad to Worse: Unemployment and Underemployment Among Less-Educated U.S.-Born Workers, 2009 to 2010," Center for Immigration Studies, August 2010. www.cis.org.

law enforcement can play an additional role through the 287(g) program. When an illegal is encountered in the normal course of police work, the immigration service should pick that person up and deport him. More agents and fencing are clearly needed at the border as well.

Harming Native Workers

As discussed above, the overall impact of immigration is almost certainly very small. It probably makes more sense for policy-makers to focus on the winners and losers from immigration. The big losers are natives working in lower-wage job jobs that require relatively little schooling. Of course, technological change and increased trade also have reduced the labor market opportunities for less-educated worker in the United States. But immigration is different because it is a discretionary policy that can be altered. On the other hand, immigrants themselves are the big winners. Owners of capital and skilled workers also make gains, though they, as made clear in this report, are tiny relative to their income.

In the end, arguments for or against immigration are as much political and moral as they are economic. The latest research indicates that we can reduce immigration secure in the knowledge that it will not harm the economy. Doing so makes sense if we are very concerned about low-wage and less-educated workers in the United States. On the other hand, if one places a high priority on helping unskilled workers in other countries, then allowing in a large number of such workers should continue. Of course, only an infinitesimal proportion of the world's poor could ever come to this country even under the most open immigration policy one might imagine. Those who support the current high level of unskilled legal and illegal immigration should at least do so with an understanding that those American workers harmed by the policies they favor are already the poorest and most vulnerable.

> "Instead of doing some thoughtful
> analysis and a bit of research, it's
> just easier to say that rising teen
> unemployment must . . . be the result
> of . . . minimum wage policies and lax
> immigration enforcement."

Neither Immigration nor the Minimum Wage Hurts the Economy

Invictus

Invictus is the pseudonym of a writer on economics and policy who blogs at The Big Picture blog. In the following viewpoint, he argues that high teen unemployment is due to neither the minimum wage nor illegal immigration. Instead, he contends, increased teen unemployment is due to an economic downturn. In particular, he asserts, the downturn has encouraged many older workers to put off retirement, forcing teen workers out of the job market. He concludes that those blaming the minimum wage or illegal immigration for teen unemployment are motivated by ideology not facts.

As you read, consider the following questions:

1. What does Invictus refer to as "easy, quick sound bites"?

2. Beside demographics, what does the author say is likely the driving factor behind high teen unemployment?

3. According to Invictus, what will cost the Obama administration dearly?

I see that in some circles illegal immigrants are now being blamed for the high teen unemployment rate. First it was the minimum wage, now it's illegals. Yawn. *This* is exactly the stuff that makes my blood boil—thoughtless, *ideologically driven bullcrap* that's presented as fact, usually without any documentary evidence. Easy, quick sound bites.

Demographics

What about demographics—an aging boomer population—and a crappy economy that has the 55-plus cohort postponing retirement and consequently crowding out the younger generation (parents keeping their own kids/grandkids out of the job market, as I put it a while back). The data is there for all who choose to explore it.

Take a good look at the chart. . . . Our demographics, coupled with a crappy economic environment, are conspiring to wreak havoc on teen employment. I really don't think there's much more to it than that. To be clear: I know there are some studies—usually authored by partisan think tanks or hacks on either side—that make both sides of minimum wage/illegals arguments. But I'd offer up two words: Occam's Razor [the idea that the simplest solution should be considered first]. And we know from the NFIB [National Federation of Independent Business] that "Poor Sales" is the single largest problem facing small businesses, so it's no surprise they're not hiring. Citing demographics—which are exceedingly difficult to spin in a political context (i.e. they are what they are and—unless you're China—generally free from policy influences)—just doesn't cut it for many folks who need to find a way to assign blame. But the various charts I've produced elsewhere and [here] provide actual, numbers-driven evidence

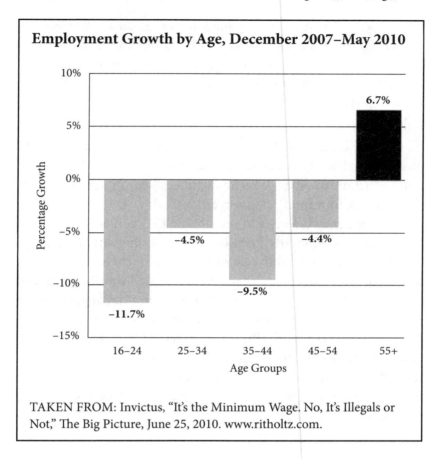

Employment Growth by Age, December 2007–May 2010

TAKEN FROM: Invictus, "It's the Minimum Wage. No, It's Illegals or Not," The Big Picture, June 25, 2010. www.ritholtz.com.

that demographics are likely the driving factor here (in addition to the fact that teens suffer disproportionately in any downturn in the first place).

What the Numbers Say

And there's also this, from an April [2010] story that appeared in the [Wall Street Journal]. It makes perfect sense, given the brutality of the job market:

> The share of new high-school graduates enrolled in college reached a record high last year, likely reflecting the weak job market they faced.

Some 70.1% of the 2.9 million new graduates between the ages of 16 and 24 headed to colleges and universities, the Labor Department said Tuesday, based on data from January through October 2009. That percentage was a historical high for the data series, which began in 1959.

But no, instead of doing some thoughtful analysis and a bit of research, it's just easier to say that rising teen unemployment must—just must!—be the result of "liberal" minimum wage policies and lax immigration enforcement.

As some may believe I'm revealing a liberal bias, I'll respond by saying that I honestly don't believe I'm doing any such thing. What I'm doing is looking at what the numbers are telling me, as evidenced by the chart [here included] and those I produced elsewhere on this topic. I'm open to discussion/debate/refutation of that data, but little has been forthcoming. And, for the record, I'll state here that I think [President Barack] Obama and his team badly misallocated the stimulus [a 2009 spending package intended to boost the economy] in ways that did little to create jobs, unarguably its most important objective. And that will cost him dearly.

Periodical and Internet
Sources Bibliography

The following articles have been selected to supplement the diverse views presented in this chapter.

Aquarian Agrarian   "Immigration and the Minimum Wage," January 29, 2011. http://aquarianagrarian.blogspot.com.

Bryan Caplan   "Immigration and the Minimum Wage," EconLog, September 19, 2010. http://econlog.econlib.org.

Tom Curry   "Will Illegal Immigration Offset a Wage Hike?," MSNBC, January 10, 2007. www.msnbc.msn.com.

Corrado Giulietti   "Is the Minimum Wage a Pull Factor for Immigrants?," Social Science Research Network, January 3, 2011. www.ssrn.org.

John Koraska   "Earned Income Tax Credit, Illegal Aliens and Minimum Wage," Debtism.com, March 25, 2005. http://debtism.com.

Paul Lazaga   "Minimum Wage Laws Foster Illegal Immigration," Paul Lazaga for Congress, April 18, 2010. www.paullazaga.org.

Tim Moreland   "Illegal Immigrants Good, Minimum Wage Bad," Associated Content, June 30, 2010. www.associatedcontent.com.

Rena Sherwood   "Illegal Immigration Does Not Cause Job Loss in America," Associated Content, March 6, 2010. www.associatedcontent.com.

George Tapinos   "Illegal Immigrants and the Labour Market," *OECD Observer*, December 1999. http://www.oecdobserver.org/news/fullstory.php/aid-190.

CHAPTER 4

What Are the Issues Surrounding the Minimum Wage in Other Countries?

Chapter Preface

On May 1, 2011, Hong Kong adopted its first-ever minimum wage. Businesses in Hong Kong must now pay employees HK$28 (US$4.70) an hour.

The minimum wage has been a longtime source of contention in Hong Kong. It was first proposed in the 1930s, but business interests, which are very powerful in the Chinese city, managed to prevent its passage for eight decades. An August 13, 2008, editorial in *China Securities Journal*, said that a minimum wage for Hong Kong was "long-overdue" and added that "setting a minimum wage can help [low-income] workers support their families and provide an improved living environment so that their children can enjoy a better chance of moving up the social ladder."

The impetus for the passage of the law was, in part, rising inequality. An April 30, 2011, article by the international news agency AFP reported that Hong Kong "is famous for its stunningly wealthy tycoons. . . . But the city is also home to hundreds of thousands of workers who live on hourly wages sometimes as low as $2 an hour." An April 30, 2011, article at the BBC's website noted that the minimum wage was "expected to benefit 270,000 low-paid workers, or around 10% of the working population."

Some commentators, however, have said that a minimum wage will hurt workers in Hong Kong. Andy Mukherjee, writing for the August 18, 2008, Bloomberg business news site, argued that Hong Kong has been impressively prosperous because of its lack of regulation and the government's refusal to meddle with the economy. "For every poor worker that would have benefited from a higher minimum wage, others would have lost their jobs," Mukherjee said. He added that "capitulation to one illiberal proposal will invariably lead to accommodation of other, more deleterious ones," and that once Hong Kong begins to regulate its economy, there could be no telling where it would stop.

The British-based *Economist* noted in a January 11, 2011, article that the minimum wage law included "requirements for holidays and annual leave tied to job tenure," which could mean that companies might fire longer-serving employees in favor of newer hires. "Unintended consequences will be rife," the newspaper predicted.

The following chapter examines minimum-wage laws and debates in other parts of the world, including Canada, Australia, China, and Bangladesh.

> "Let's keep the raises coming for the lowest paid among [Canadians]. It's good for them, and it's good for the labour market."

Raising the Minimum Wage in Canada Helps the Poor and the Economy

Jim Stanford

Jim Stanford is an economist with the Canadian autoworkers' union. In the following viewpoint he asserts that minimum wages in Canada have been rising in recent years. He contends that this is sound policy and that higher minimum wages have a negligible effect on increasing unemployment. They also boost productivity and increase labor-force attachment, he maintains. He concludes that the minimum wage should be increased further to help low-income workers and the Canadian economy.

As you read, consider the following questions:

1. Besides Ontario, what other provinces does Stanford say are raising the minimum wage?
2. How much have real average hourly wages in Canada

grown in the three years ending in 2009, and why does the author believe this is significant?

3. To what level does Stanford say the minimum wage should be increased?

Raise a glass today [March 30, 2010,] in honour of the hard-working souls who flip burgers, serve double-doubles and clean hotel rooms. In Ontario, they just got a decent raise: the minimum wage goes up 75 cents, to $10.25 an hour. That makes Ontario's minimum the highest in Canada—and today marks the first time the bottom rung of our labour market passes that $10 threshold.

Wages Rising

The new benchmark represents the completion of a promise made by the [Dalton] McGuinty government [of Ontario] in 2007. Since then, minimum wage workers in Ontario have pocketed 28 per cent in wage increases. At the time, Queen's Park [the seat of government in Ontario] was feeling pressure from a feisty grassroots campaign, led by the Toronto Labour Council, for a $10 minimum. Now their hope is a reality (even if it took three years to get there).

The Ontario move is worth celebrating. But just as encouraging, other provinces are joining the effort to boost the fortunes of the lowest paid. Newfoundland's minimum wage will reach $10 this July [2010], as will New Brunswick's next fall. Most other provinces, rich and poor alike, are already at $9 or higher.

On average, Canadian minimum wages have increased 20 per cent in the past three years. That's significantly faster than inflation—hence, boosting the real purchasing power of minimum wage workers. But it's not just them who benefit. Many other low-wage jobs are paid at specified increments above the minimum wage, so those workers also get a raise.

This "trickle up" effect helps explain recent increases in real average hourly wages in Canada. In the three years ending in

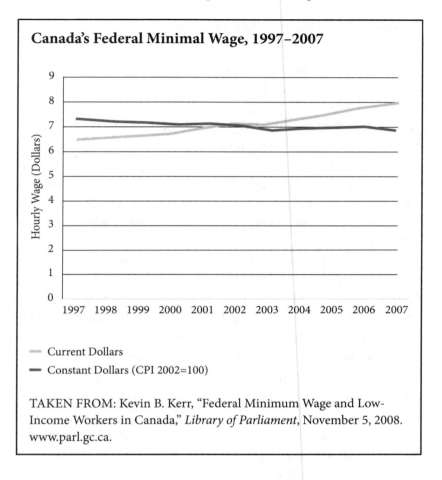

Canada's Federal Minimal Wage, 1997–2007

Current Dollars

Constant Dollars (CPI 2002=100)

TAKEN FROM: Kevin B. Kerr, "Federal Minimum Wage and Low-Income Workers in Canada," *Library of Parliament*, November 5, 2008. www.parl.gc.ca.

2009, average wages (after adjusting for inflation) grew by 4 per cent. That's not a lot—but it's the best wage performance for Canadian workers since the 1970s. The unheralded revitalization of minimum wage policy is a big reason why.

This rebound reverses the trend of previous decades. In 1976, the average minimum wage in Canada was $2.65 an hour. At today's consumer prices, that's the equivalent of almost $10. But then governments allowed minimum wages to erode, falling far behind inflation. By 1991, the real value of minimum wages had been cut by a third (to less than $7 an hour, in today's terms). And there they languished, for another decade or more.

Benefits Outweigh Disadvantages

At that time, many economists believed that minimum wages create unemployment, by "interfering" with market mechanisms and preventing "less productive" workers from getting a job. But it turned out those economists were wrong. A new generation of minimum wage researchers discovered that the disemployment effects of graduated minimum wage increases are negligible (even in nasty industries such as fast-food restaurants). And the spinoff benefits of higher minimums (including stronger labour-force attachment by marginalized groups, and pressure on low-wage employers to boost productivity) are considerable.

But not all provincial governments have rediscovered minimum wage religion. Since taking office, B.C. [British Columbia] Premier Gordon Campbell has taken his province from champ to chump in the low-wage sweepstakes. In 2001, B.C. had Canada's highest minimum wage ($8). Today, it's the lowest—still $8. In that time, inflation eroded the purchasing power of B.C. minimum wage workers by almost 20 per cent; Mr. Campbell made things worse with a new super-low minimum of $6 for new hires.

In free-market theory, this should have made B.C. a nirvana for low-wage workers (especially young people). In reality, B.C.'s tight-fisted approach didn't stop youth employment from falling faster, and the youth unemployment rate from rising further, than any other province as the recession hit in 2009. So much for the virtues of a flexible "free market."

The recent rebound in minimum wages still hasn't fixed the damage from decades of neglect. In real terms, the average minimum is still a dollar lower than in 1976. And relative to average hourly productivity, minimum wages have continued to shrink. Today's minimum wages equal just 15 per cent of the output produced by the typical Canadian worker in an hour's work. Therefore, to help low-wage workers capture the same share of output as they did in the 1970s, minimum wages should be increased to $12.50 an hour. To bring low-wage workers up to the poverty line, it should go higher.

So let's keep the raises coming for the lowest paid among us. It's good for them, and it's good for the labour market.

"Raising the minimum wage results in
. . . wiping out the jobs held by those
the advocates of the measure claim they
want to help."

Raising the Minimum Wage in Canada Will Hurt Those It Is Meant to Help

Harvey Enchin

Harvey Enchin is a columnist and economic commentator for the Vancouver Sun. In the following viewpoint, he argues that raising the minimum wage will cause an increase in unemployment and will fuel inflation. He says that unions push for an increase in the minimum wage so that union workers will not have to compete with lower-paid workers for the same jobs. Enchin argues that most minimum-wage workers are young people or women who do not rely on their wages for a living. He concludes that minimum-wage hikes hurt the economy and do little to help the poor.

As you read, consider the following questions:

1. What does Enchin say would happen if the minimum wage were raised to $100?

2. According to the author, how many British Columbians earned minimum wage or less in 2006?

3. What evidence does Enchin point to in order to show that most workers do not earn the minimum wage for long?

It's comforting to believe we can alleviate poverty by simply raising the minimum wage.

That's the myth driving the British Columbia Federation of Labour's [BC Fed/the Fed] campaign to raise the minimum wage to $10 from $8, the level set in 2001 and since matched by five other provinces.

But the union movement's purpose isn't altruistic. Its hidden agenda is to price the competition out of the market. By narrowing the gap between the cost of hiring low-skilled, minimum wage workers and unionized workers, unions hope to squeeze them out and replace them at higher wages with their minions.

Employment opportunities for the lowest paid dwindle while job openings for card-carrying, dues-paying members increase. If some minimum wage jobs disappear as a result of businesses choosing, in order to avoid the increased cost of labour, to either not do the work, or close up shop, only minimum wage workers are hurt.

Research has repeatedly found that raising the minimum wage results in net employment losses, wiping out the jobs held by those the advocates of the measure claim they want to help.

Studies of the impact of minimum wage laws over 50 years haven't found any evidence to support the contention that raising the minimum wage reduces poverty. In fact, the adverse impacts of minimum wage increases are well documented. If raising the minimum wage had the effects its proponents claim, we could eliminate the scourge of poverty by mandating all nations to increase theirs.

And why to just $10? Why not $50, or $100? This is nonsense, of course, because economies would adjust to the inflated value of labour by inflating the price of everything else, leaving no one better off—just as our economy will if politicians in [BC's capital city] Victoria or elsewhere buy into the falsehood that they can help the poor by raising the minimum wage.

And the Fed's claim is false. It has even misrepresented the numbers of workers at this income level to try to make its case.

It argues that 115,000 British Columbians earn the minimum wage and another 135,000 earn less than $10. However, Statistics Canada [StatsCan] reports that in 2006 only 4.6 per cent of employed workers, or roughly 82,000, earned minimum wage or less.

The union propagandists claim the proportion of workers earning minimum wage or less is growing under the Liberal government when, in fact, after an uptick in 2002—the lag effect of misguided policies of the New Democrats during the decade of decline in the 1990s—the proportion has returned to historic levels and has remained relatively stable.

Minimum Wage Is for the Young

The chief reason raising the minimum wage won't help the poor is that minimum wage workers aren't who the BC Fed says they are. They are not the breadwinners of the "working families" the NDP [Canada's social democrat party] claims to represent, the illusory "class" the left had to invent to feed its Marxist fantasy of class struggle.

Nearly 60 per cent of those earning the minimum wage or less are young people and two-thirds are women. Most of the young are still living at home and their employment income is not their sole means of support. Similarly, most of the women cohabit with a primary income earner. Neither live in households falling below StatsCan's low-income cutoff. Raising the minimum wage might indeed increase the income of these groups, providing assistance not to those who need it most but to middle- and upper-income households that do not depend on this income.

Another fact is that about 14 per cent of workers who didn't make it through high school earn the minimum wage compared with less than three per cent of those with some post-secondary education. Gosh, workers who go to the trouble of getting more education make more money. Who could've guessed?

Finally, the statistics reveal another concealed truth. Few workers earn the minimum wage for long.

In 2006, 10 per cent of workers who had been in their current jobs for a year or less earned the minimum wage or less. Workers in the same job for one to five years were half as likely to earn the minimum wage and those employed for five years or more in the same position were 10 times less likely to earn the minimum wage.

A single study in 1995 by economists David Card and Alan Krueger purports to show that an increase in the minimum wage does not increase unemployment and is widely cited by the left, but it remains a lone contrarian thesis in a sea of peer-reviewed economic studies that prove the opposite.

Policy-makers must recognize the political and economic motives of the union movement's minimum wage campaign and review the research that shows raising the minimum wage will do nothing to reduce poverty but rather will eliminate low-wage jobs and fuel inflation, eroding the purchasing power of the working class and everyone else.

> *"The [Australian] government is only worried that minimum wages have fallen so low that jobless workers could actually be better off on unemployment benefits."*

Australia Must Raise the Minimum Wage Higher

Noel Holt

Noel Holt was a worker for Telstra mobile phone company and a Socialist Equality Party parliamentary candidate in Australia. In the following viewpoint, he argues that a 2010 increase in the minimum wage in Australia was insufficient and that the real value of the minimum wage has stagnated for two decades. In that time, he maintains, inequality has widened, and the richest have made huge profits. He blames the government and the unions for failing to do more to distribute prosperity to low-income workers.

As you read, consider the following questions:

1. What does Holt say the minimum wage per week will be after the increase, and how much of an increase is that per hour?

2. What groups of the rich were doing the best in Australia,

Noel Holt, "Minimum Pay Ruling Deepens Social Inequality," World Socialist Web Site, June 8, 2010. Copyright © 2010 World Socialist Web Site. wsws.org. All rights reserved. Reprinted with permission.

according to the *BRW* Rich 200 list that the author cites?

3. Who does Holt say is directly responsible for the worsening plight of poorly paid workers?

D espite media claims of a victory for low-paid workers, the $26 a week rise in the minimum wage awarded by the [prime minister Kevin] Rudd government's Fair Work Australia (FWA) tribunal last week [early June 2010], is actually a further real wage cut, after a two-year freeze. The 4.8 percent increase is below the official Consumer Price Index, which has risen 5.4 percent over the past 21 months since the last rise.

More Needed

The Australian Council of Trade Unions (ACTU) welcomed the outcome, absurdly claiming it would "restore some equity and fairness into our economy". The ACTU claim was for only a dollar more—$27 a week—despite welfare groups submitting that the rise needed to be $49 a week, or 9 percent, just to make up the cuts inflicted by the previous [John] Howard government's Australian Fair Pay Commission.

About 1.4 million award-dependent workers are affected by the FWA ruling, including about 100,000 on the National Minimum Wage, which will rise to $15 an hour. They are the country's worst-paid workers—including child care workers, shop assistants, cafe and restaurant workers, labourers, office staff and cleaners.

The minimum wage will be $569.90 per week, an increase of just 69 cents per hour. As many low-paid workers commented to the media, this will hardly make any difference to their financial difficulties. Joy Stevens, a case worker with a charity organisation who is paid just above the minimum wage, said the decision would only provide for the little things, such as to "budget for a coffee or a couple of DVDs". Margarita Murray-Stark, a Melbourne hotel cleaner on $15.41 an hour, told the *Australian*: "$26 is still not enough. When you have a look, it's nothing." She pointed to rising mortgage interest rates and public transport fares.

Many struggling single income households will get much less than $26. A single person on the minimum wage (working 38 hours a week) will receive $22 after paying tax, while a single income household receiving parenting payments for children will take home as little as $6.50 after paying tax and losing parenting payments at the rate of 60 cents on the dollar.

Employer groups, whose members benefited from last year's wage freeze, denounced the decision as "extreme" and warned of job losses. Victorian Employers Chamber of Commerce and Industry spokesperson Alexandra Marriott, for example, made it clear the organisation wanted wages suppressed for even longer. "Now is not the time to be playing catch-up," she said.

A Sharp Decline

Data in the FWA decision underlines the sharp decline in the position of low-paid workers over the past three decades. The minimum wage fell in real terms during the 1980s and early 1990s. Although it rose moderately from the mid-1990s, its real value is roughly the same now as it was 20 years ago. Those workers just slightly above the minimum wage fared worse. Between 1999 and 2010, wages for those "at the higher end of the low paid spectrum" declined in real terms by up to 15.7 percent.

The gap between the low paid and high income earners has widened dramatically. The ratio of the adult minimum wage to full-time median earnings declined from 61.9 percent in 1997 to 54.4 percent in 2008. These figures do not show the even larger gap that has opened up with the wealthiest layers of society, which have profited from the Rudd government's stimulus packages to boost the banks and businesses.

According to the recently published *BRW* [Business Review Weekly] Rich 200 list, after a sluggish year for wealth in 2009, Australia's richest people have "bounced back in style" this year, adding more than $21 billion to their collective fortune. The list's

Minimum Wage's Origins in Australia

The minimum wage has been a core element of public policy for more than a century. Originating in the 1890s in New Zealand and Australia, minimum wages spread to the United Kingdom in 1909 and to nearly one-third of U.S. states during the next two decades. In 1938, the U.S. Congress passed a federal minimum wage law as part of the Fair Labor Standards Act. Since that time, minimum wages have been introduced in some form or another in numerous other industrialized countries, as well as in some developing countries. As a result, by the 1990s, minimum wages existed in well over one hundred countries from all parts of the world, and the International Labour Organization (ILO) has designated the minimum wage as an international labor standard.

David Neumark and William L. Wascher,
Minimum Wages, *2008.*

total wealth rose from $114 billion to almost $136 billion, with property and mining magnates doing the best. Twenty-five mine owners increased their worth by about $9 billion between them.

The past decade has also seen a sharp rise in the proportion of workers on low pay, defined as less than two-thirds of median earnings. The incidence of low-paid employment increased from 10.6 percent of all employees in 2003 to 14.6 percent in 2007.

This process has been accompanied by an unprecedented surge in productivity and therefore profit rates. Over the past decade, GDP [gross domestic product] per hour worked rose by 16 percent, and in the market sector it rose by 20 percent. This compares with the 2.4 percent growth in the real value of the minimum wage and falls in the real value of award wages over the same period.

Deputy Prime Minister Julia Gillard said she was pleased by the pay ruling, saying that the increase of around $6 a week above inflation would "no doubt be welcomed by those who are paying their mortgage or rents, and buying the family groceries". Last year, she urged workers to accept the pay freeze imposed by the Fair Pay Commission because it was an "independent industrial umpire".

Better Off on Unemployment

Far from being concerned for the low-paid, the Rudd government is only worried that minimum wages have fallen so low that jobless workers could actually be better off on unemployment benefits—which the government has deliberately kept near official poverty rates. The government asked the FWA to ensure that the minimum wage rose just enough to ensure there remained "financial incentives" for people to "enter paid work".

The FWA tribunal members also noted that the increase would help offset the government's "award modernisation" process, due to take general effect on July 1 [2010], which would lead to pay cuts for many low-paid workers. "We are also aware that the modern awards will bring significant benefits for many employers, including some reductions in minimum wages, penalty rates and other conditions".

Politically, the decision assists the unions, giving them a "victory" to justify the campaign they have launched for the government's re-election this year. ACTU secretary Jeff Lawrence claimed that the pay ruling marked the final end of the Howard government's WorkChoices era. The ACTU is currently running media ads claiming that Labor's "Fair Work Australia" laws have ended the anti-worker provisions of the WorkChoices legislation, despite the fact that all the measures outlawing industrial action remain.

Lawrence said the pay decision "gives low-paid workers a dividend from the federal government's successful handling of the global financial crisis and its new Fair Work laws". In reality, in its submissions to the tribunal, the ACTU was at pains to assure the FWA that a rise of this size would not dampen profits. The ACTU submitted that its claim for a $27 per week increase "adds a negligible 0.30 percent to ordinary time earnings and a barely measurable CPI [consumer price index; that is, the price of consumer goods] impact of 0.16 percent."

For decades, the ACTU and its affiliates have helped the employers and successive governments to isolate and suppress struggles for better pay and conditions. They are directly responsible for the worsening plight of the expanding army of poorly-paid workers.

> *"The wage rise will be a dangerous setback to economic recovery in the small business sector."*

Raising Australia's Minimum Wage Will Hurt Businesses

PM

PM is a radio news program on ABC, the Australian public broadcasting station. In the following viewpoint taken from a PM transcript, PM reporters and interviewees contend that an increase in the Australian minimum wage put through in 2010 is opposed by business groups. The government agency responsible for the increase, Fair Work Australia, says the change should not hurt the economy. Business groups, however, say the minimum wage increase is too high, especially in a recession, and that it may cause inflation, threaten businesses, and cost jobs.

As you read, consider the following questions:

1. Why does the ACTU's Jeff Lawrence, as quoted on *PM*, say a pay raise is reasonable?
2. What industries does Greg Evans, as quoted on *PM*, say will be hit hardest by the wage increase?
3. What does Russell Zimmerman, as quoted on *PM*, say he

"Business Groups Say Minimum Pay Increase Will Damage Employment," *PM*, June 3, 2010. www.abc.net.au/pm. Copyright © 2010 by ABC. All rights reserved. Reproduced by permission of the Australian Broadcasting Corporation and ABC Online.

is worried about for his own business with the increase in the minimum wage?

*M*ark *Colvin*: Business groups are furious with a decision by the Federal Government's new industrial umpire to award Australia's lowest paid workers a $26 a week pay rise.

People on the minimum wage are celebrating their first pay rise in about two years.

Fair Work Australia says the increase won't threaten business viability, inflation or employment.

But employers say the increase is risky, irresponsible, unjustified and will cost jobs.

As Simon Lauder reports, Fair Work Australia has also indicated that it's leaning towards a new way of adjusting the minimum wage.

Simon Lauder: From next month [July 2010] the new minimum wage will be about $570 a week, just $1 shy of the amount the Australian Council of Trade Unions [ACTU] was pushing for.

At an ACTU press conference to respond to the announcement, Canberra childcare worker, Janelle Keenan, says she's struggled to make ends meet, after last year's minimum wage freeze.

Janelle Keenan: We've got a mortgage and at the end of the fortnight [two-week period] we don't have much left at all, so at least it'll be nice to have a little bit left over to try and save and to take a step further to start a family.

Lauder: Fair Work Australia says the increase is no threat to the economy while company profits, wages and employment are all on the up.

The ACTU's Jeff Lawrence says today's decision provides catch up pay for about 1½ million workers who've had no pay rise for two years.

Jeff Lawrence: It recognises the fact that there's been a wage freeze, so people have been so disadvantaged that they haven't kept up with inflation and that needs to be compensated. And I think the other point is that it recognises that in this country we've got a tradition of sustaining minimum wages and sharing productivity and prosperity and that's what this decision goes a long way to do.

Lauder: The Deputy Prime Minister and Workplace Relations Minister Julia Gillard has dismissed concerns the pay rise will put pressure on inflation and employment growth.

Julia Gillard: I'd refer people to yesterday's national accounts; and what those national accounts figures are telling you is that through the action that was taken when we were faced with the global financial crisis, that we've supported jobs.

Lauder: The Australian Chamber of Commerce and Industry is pointing to those same figures to explain its concern that the wage rise will be a dangerous setback to economic recovery in the small business sector.

The Chamber's Greg Evans says the wage rise is irresponsible.

Beyond Fair and Reasonable

Greg Evans: We're not opposed to a fair and reasonable increase in the minimum wage but this goes beyond both those measures.

Lauder: Mr. Evans says the rise will add $2.5 billion to the annual wages bill of Australian small business. He says retail, hospitality and tourism will be hit the hardest.

Evans: If you look at yesterday's national accounts these are the areas in particular that are suffering very low demand conditions at the moment. This decision today is going to have consequence in terms of restoring hours worked amongst employees; we saw in the global financial downturn that many hours of work actually deteriorated.

The other impact of this decision is that it will impact on new entrants to the labour market, particularly younger workers entering into the labour market.

Lauder: The Australian Industry Group describes the wage decision as risky at a time when employers are still dealing with the effects of the global downturn and consumer confidence is weakening.

The head of the Australian Retailers Association, Russell Zimmerman, says retailers are reeling at the decision which comes at the same time as businesses are preparing for some greater costs because of the Federal Government's shake-up of award conditions.

Russell Zimmerman: For example, in New South Wales you've got a situation occurring whereby on Saturday you were paying normal pay plus loading, now you're paying time-and-a-half and on Sunday it's going from time-and-a-half to double time.

Lauder: What's your own experience; you're a small business man, what are you worried about?

Zimmerman: Yeah, look, we've got a couple of retail stores, we've got about 15 staff in total; some of those staff are paid on the award, some of them are paid over the award, so we're going to have to look at that and decide whether we have to make the ones that are over the award absorb it. Obviously those that are on the award we'll have to pay the increase; we may need to look at whether we can keep those staff on the same hours as what they were.

Lauder: The $26 a week means a lot to those on the lowest pay, but there are many others working for award wages who won't notice the increase as much.

In its decision today, Fair Work Australia notes that making increases in dollar amounts across the board erodes the value of wage increases for people on higher award rates. It says there's a strong case to start making adjustments in percentage terms instead.

Flinders University labour market researcher, Dr. Josh Healy, says workers who would benefit from an award wage increase in percentage terms include professionals such as engineers.

Josh Healy: The fact is that their wages have been declining in real terms, and that's been happening at the same time as workers of a similar class, doing similar types of jobs, in the bargaining sector have seen their wages racing ahead.

So long as we continue with this practice of awarding dollar increases, those employers will continue to be able to employ these higher skilled workers at fairly modest cost.

Lauder: Fair Work Australia says more research needs to be done on the impact of a percentage wage increase on costs and employment.

"*Hundreds of workers gathered in downtown Cairo . . ., demanding that the government implement the court order [to raise the minimum wage].*"

Demand for an Increased Minimum Wage Triggered Protests in Egypt

Joel Beinin

Joel Beinin is a professor of Middle East history at Stanford University and the principal author of The Struggle for Worker Rights in Egypt. *In the following viewpoint, he reports that in early 2010 Egyptian workers held a rally demanding an increase in the minimum wage. These protests, Beinin says, were so intense that the government called out security forces to intimidate protesters. Beinin argues that wages in Egypt are so low that many Egyptians are too poor to afford food or other necessities and concludes that the protests may result in an autocratic crackdown.*

As you read, consider the following questions:

1. What is the ETFU, as described by Beinin?
2. What is the typical monthly wage of textile workers in

families with two wage earners, according to the author?

3. What impact does Beinin believe the minimum wage protests may have on the upcoming parliamentary elections in Egypt?

O n May 11 [2010] the Egyptian government extended the State of Emergency, which has been in effect continuously since 1981, for an additional two years. The Emergency Law gives the regime broad powers which it has used to try to suppress dissent of all sorts. But the law and other repressive measures have been ineffective in stemming the tidal wave of public protests by workers and others that have severely eroded the legitimacy of the regime of President Hosni Mubarak.

Working-Class Dissent

Since February workers from over a dozen workplaces have sat-in nearly continuously in front of Egypt's parliament. Each group has its own demands related to wages and working conditions in their workplace. Collectively, they have established a permanent presence of working-class dissent in downtown Cairo targeting the neoliberal economic policies the government headed by Prime Minister Ahmad Nazif has implemented with renewed vigor since taking office in July 2004.

The success of the sit-in tactic was established in December 2007, when 3,000 municipal real estate tax collectors occupied the street in front of the Ministry of Finance for 11 days. They won a 325% salary increase; and their action led to creating the first independent trade union since the government-controlled Egyptian Trade Union Federation (ETUF) was established in 1957.

Since 1998 over 2 million workers have participated in more than 3,300 factory occupations, strikes, demonstrations, or other collective actions protesting low wages, non-payment of bonuses, wage supplements, and social benefits, and private investors' failure to uphold their contractual obligations to their workers.

Revolution in Egypt

An 18-day-old revolt led by the young people of Egypt ousted President Hosni Mubarak on Friday [February 11, 2011] shattering three decades of political stasis here and overturning the established order of the Arab world.

Shouts of "God is great" erupted from Tahrir Square at twilight as Mr. Mubarak's vice president and longtime intelligence chief, Omar Suleiman, announced that Mr. Mubarak had passed all authority to a council of military leaders.

David D. Kirkpatrick, New York Times,
February 11, 2011.

The protests spiked sharply since the Nazif government accelerated the pace of privatization of public-sector enterprises in 2004. According to a recent report published by the Solidarity Center, *The Struggle for Worker Rights in Egypt*, privatization has usually meant less job security, longer hours, and a lower standard of social services for workers, while ETUF rarely defends their interests.

The character of worker protests has been changing since late March. Supported by NGOs [nongovernmental organizations] like the Center for Trade Union and Workers Services and the recently established Egyptian Center for Economic and Social Rights, a growing number of workers are coalescing around the demand for a national monthly minimum wage of 1,200 Egyptian pounds (about $215). That proposal was first advanced in 2008 by workers at the giant Misr Spinning and Weaving Co., in the Nile Delta. Security forces prevented Misr workers from striking in support of this demand on April 8, 2008.

The demand for a living minimum wage was revived when Nagi Rashad, a worker at the South Cairo Grain Mill and a leading figure in the workers' protest movement, sued the government over its 2008 decision not to increase the national minimum wage. The basic monthly minimum wage, equivalent to about $6.35 at the current exchange rate, was established in 1984. With cost of living increases, it reached nearly $25.00 in 2008. Bonuses and supplements to the basic wage—if they are paid— make it difficult to calculate actual wages precisely. Khaled 'Ali, director of the Egyptian Center for Economic and Social Rights, was the lead attorney on Rashad's case. On March 30 he won an administrative court ruling ordering the president, the prime minister, and the National Council for Wages to set a "fair" minimum wage reflecting the current cost of living.

Inadequate Pay

Wages of most Egyptian workers are inadequate to pay for food, clothing, shelter, and education. Even with two wage earners, the typical monthly wage of textile workers, which ranges from $45–$107 a month, is below the World Bank's poverty line of $2 a day for the average Egyptian family of 3.7 people. According to the World Bank, nearly 44 percent of Egyptians are "extremely poor" (unable to meet minimum food needs), "poor" (unable to meet basic food needs), or "near-poor" (able to meet some basic food needs).

On April 3 workers rallied in Cairo while a delegation sought to present a copy of the court ruling ordering the government to implement a minimum wage to cabinet members. After cabinet representatives refused to meet with them, they called another demonstration to support a national monthly minimum wage of 1,200 Egyptian pounds for May 2. Hundreds of workers gathered in downtown Cairo that day, demanding that the government implement the court order. They were confronted by a massive deployment of security forces attempting to intimidate them.

Protesters chanted "A fair minimum wage, or let this government go home" and "Down with Mubarak and all those who raise prices!" Khaled 'Ali told the press, "The government represents the marriage between authority and money—and this marriage needs to be broken up."

The court order, which the government is loathe to implement fearing that it will reduce foreign investment, and the potential for a workers movement united around a single national demand apparently unsettled the regime. President Mubarak, who had not appeared in public since undergoing gall bladder surgery in March, made a rare Cairo appearance to address a tame audience of ETUF officials about the rising tide of protest. "There is no place at this critical stage for those who can't distinguish between change and chaos," he said. This has been Mubarak's traditional gambit at home and to his western patrons whenever democratic demands are raised—better the autocracy you know than instability. This may signal that the parliamentary elections scheduled for later this year will be even less free and fair than those of 2005.

| "Wage increases . . . could . . . fuel inflation."

China's Increase of Its Minimum Wages May Fuel Inflation

Moming Zhou

Moming Zhou is a MarketWatch reporter in San Franciso. In the following viewpoint Zhou reports that inflation in China is increasing. As a result, individuals and families can purchase less, which authorities fear may contribute to social unrest. To prevent such unrest, Zhou reports, China is raising the minimum wage. But there is concern that increasing the minimum wage will in turn fuel further inflation, as businesses pass on increased costs to consumers.

As you read, consider the following questions:

1. By how much did Tibet raise minimum wages at the beginning of 2008, according to Zhou?
2. How much of China's economic output is produced by Guangdong, according to the author?
3. As described by Zhou, what is Haier?

In an effort to calm grousing consumers as prices rise to 11-year highs, China is raising minimum wages across the country, a move analysts fear could further stoke inflation.

Guangdong, China's richest province, said it plans to raise minimum wages by as much as 18% in some cities starting April 1. The decision followed similar actions in other areas, notably the major cities of Shanghai and Beijing. Tibet, an autonomous region administered by China's central government, raised minimum wages by nearly 50% at the beginning of this year.

The wage increases, aimed at relieving food and other price pressures, could instead fuel inflation, analysts said. Higher wages are also likely to raise prices of U.S. imports from China, and possibly reduce China's attraction as the world's manufacturing center. China is wrestling with consumer inflation that accelerated to 7.1% in January, up from a 6.5% rise in December, the National Bureau of Statistics reported last week. See full story. As an example of higher prices, McDonald Corp's (MCD 75.09, -0.16, -0.21%) China stores recently raised the chain's Big Mac price to 12 yuan ($1.70), up 14% from just seven months ago, reflecting higher meat and wheat prices.

In December, Kentucky Fried Chicken, owned by Yum! Brands Inc. (YUM 51.78, -0.06, -0.12%), also raised prices in its China stores for the first time in more than three years.

China's Dilemma

Since last year, Chinese residents have seen prices of food and other staples increase more than their pay checks, a factor analysts said could potentially unleash social unrest. In light of that, some fear the minimum wage increase came too late.

"It's a dilemma for China," said David Riedel, president of overseas-stock specialist Riedel Research Group. "The reality of higher food and fuel prices has to be offset with higher wages. This is more wages catching up to where the market is today."

The wage increases could feed inflation, he said, explaining that companies absorbing higher wages have to pass those costs

Inflation Rate in China, 2008–2010

China's inflation fell in late 2008–09 when the global financial crisis hit. In 2010–11 it began to rise again.

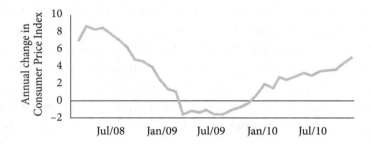

TAKEN FROM: Lumpy Investor, "China's Inflation Starting to Spike—Investors Beware," January 3, 2011. http://lumpyinvestor.blogspot.com.

onto their customers. Guangdong will increase the province's minimum wages by an average 13% on April 1, the province's labor bureau said in a news release. The southern China province produces about 13% of China's economic output, the most among the country's 32 provinces.

Minimum wages in the capital city Guangzhou will rise to 860 yuan ($120) per month from 780 yuan, an increase of 10%. Wages of other cities in the province will also get a boost, with those in some inland cities up nearly 18%.

China's other provinces took similar actions earlier this year. Starting Jan. 1, four provinces hiked their average minimum wages by more than 20%, with the increase in Tibet topping the list, according to data collected by Citigroup. Five other provinces increased average wage caps by more than 10%.

Beijing and Shanghai, China's two biggest cities, last year raised their minimum wages to 730 yuan and 840 yuan, respectively, in the face of rising consumer prices.

Average minimum wages in China have risen 15% in 2007, Citigroup said in a report, and 21% in 2008 based on available data.

Higher Inflation

The wage hike came as some analysts were already reconsidering their estimates for Chinese inflation.

"The current consensus view is that this year's inflation should peak in the first quarter," said Lan Xue, an analyst at Citigroup, in a separate research note. However, Xue said "we are getting nervous that not only may we not see a moderation in the second quarter," but that inflation could even continue rising into second half or even 2009. Recent inflation has even spread to home appliances, one of the most oversupplied goods in China.

Haier, China's biggest appliance producers and an exporter of mini refrigerators and other appliances, said it will raise domestic prices of refrigerators and washing machines by 7% to 10% in response to higher production costs.

The price rises are notable because winter is usually the slowest season for selling appliances, according to Citi's Xue, who added that it is "probably the first time in the past 15 years that we have seen price increases" in that sector.

Guangdong province, whose minimum wages will be the country's highest as of April, is China's largest manufacturing center for home appliances. That could put even more upward pressure on appliance prices.

| *"The government has openly
acknowledged that the minimum wage
was uncompetitive."*

Ireland Must Lower All Wages to Regain Economic Competitiveness

Fionnuala Carolan

Fionnuala Carolan is the editor of ShelfLife, *a magazine for the grocery and convenience store sectors in Ireland. In the following viewpoint, she argues that Ireland's minimum wage has long been too high. Especially in light of the economic crisis in Ireland in 2008–2011, she argues that wages need to fall to reduce unemployment and help businesses. She notes that the government has reduced the minimum wage in most industries; however, in retail and other sectors covered by the legally established Joint Labour Committee (JLC), minimum wages are to be increased. Carolan argues that minimum wages for all workers must be reduced for Ireland to regain an economic edge.*

As you read, consider the following questions:

1. Before the minimum wage reduction, according to Carolon, where did Ireland's minimum wage fall among

all European minimum wages? What about after the minimum wage reduction?

2. What does the author say is the unemployment rate in Ireland, and how many people are unemployed?

3. By how much does the JLC mandate that wages must increase in January 2011, according to Carolan?

It's been a strange month but then I suppose it's a fitting end to an equally strange year [2010]. While it is laughable that we were assured by the government this time last year that the worst [of Ireland's financial crisis] was over, things have managed to get progressively worse as the year has dragged on.

A Burden to Employers

The past month [November–December] has seen the IMF [International Monetary Fund] descend on the country and burden us with a bailout package we can't afford to pay back, we've encountered some of the most severe weather many of us have ever seen at this most crucial time of the year for the retail industry and we've experienced a truly harsh budget.

One of the most significant developments of the budget was the introduction of the Financial Emergency Measures Bill which reduced the minimum wage by one euro to €7.65 an hour. This means we no longer have the second highest minimum wage in Europe. We now sit in fifth place, which is slightly more respectable.

The minimum wage was considered far too high for far too long and it had become a huge burden to employers. Although the new rate will seem harsh to those on the minimum wage it is still over 8% higher than the UK rate of £5.93 (€7.06). Most employees would prefer to have a job at the minimum wage than not to have one at all, a likely scenario as employers are forced to cut staff numbers due to unsustainable wage bills.

We have an unemployment rate of 13.6% (438,800 people now unemployed) so we needed to do something to stem the

---

JLC/REA Rates of Pay

Contract Cleaning	€9.50/hour as of 6/1/2008
Agricultural Worker	€8.65/hour as of 1/7/2011
Retail Grocery	€7.67/hour as of 6/1/2011
Security Industry	€10.01/hour as of 1/1/2009

TAKEN FROM: "List of JLC/REA Rates of Pay," http://www
.labourcourt.ie./labour/labour.nsf/LookupPageLink/RatesofPay.

---

numbers of young people leaving these shores to seek employment abroad.

So you would imagine that employers of small businesses would be delighted by this turn of events. Well unfortunately not all of them can celebrate. In the retail, hospitality and cleaning sectors, the decrease in the minimum wage means diddly squat due to the continual enforcement of the Joint Labour Committee[1] pay rates.

Now there is an even greater divide between minimum rates of pay and that of those in the industries with JLC agreements in place ensuring that employers in these sectors are at a distinct disadvantage to other sectors. There is now an 18% difference between the new minimum wage and the JLC rates for the retail sector. What's even worse is that the proposed JLC increase set for January [2011] is still due to go ahead.

From 1 January 2011 employers can expect to pay an extra 1.25% on already inflated wages and it is proposed that from 1 June 2011 they will increase it by yet another 1.25%.

Out of Sync with Rest of Europe

Our overall rates of pay in Ireland have long been out of sync with the rest of Europe and considering the state of our economy something needed to be done to rectify this. Even with the drop in the minimum wage it still seems wrong to have the fifth highest minimum wage in Europe.

We have to be practical and make this country a viable place to do business again but surely the same rules should apply for all employers. IBEC [Irish Business and Employers Confederation] has said that regaining competitiveness and getting Irish labour costs back into line with similar economies is central to economic recovery.

Director General of RGDATA [the representative organisation for independent family grocers in Ireland], Tara Buckley described the JLC agreements as "antiquated" and explained that for the sake of job preservation, we need to abolish JCLs entirely. RGDATA has been in discussions with the government over the past month about changing or abolishing the JLC agreements but they are now waiting to hear the recommendations of these discussions and there is no time frame in which this is set to happen.

All of the arguments pertaining to the cut in minimum wage make sense. So why then are these draconian JLC rates still in place when the government has openly acknowledged that the minimum wage was uncompetitive? This needs to change immediately.

This year has seen many businesses truly tested and the weather conditions during prime shopping season was just another blow. However the next couple of weeks will be the busiest of the year so make sure you do all you can to keep your loyal customers coming back through your door next year.

Note

1. The Joint Labour Committee in Ireland is an independent body set up by statutory order that regulates pay rates in certain industries.

| "I am generally in favour of a minimum
wage, even in Bangladesh."

A Higher Minimum Wage Could Benefit Bangladesh

Sajjadur Rahman and Brendan Weston

Sajjadur Rahman and Brendan Weston are reporters for the Bangladesh Daily Star. *In the following viewpoint, they report on a discussion with British economist Alan Manning. Manning argues that increasing the minimum wage often does not result in as many job losses as predicted. He contends that increasing minimum wage reduces employee turnover and can encourage investment in technology, both of which can lead to higher productivity. Manning says that a minimum wage, if properly enforced and set at a reasonable rate, can improve the lot of workers without hurting business even in developing countries like Bangladesh.*

As you read, consider the following questions:

1. In what way is the Latin American experience with the minimum wage a cautionary tale, according to Alan Manning, as cited by the authors?
2. Why does Manning, according to Rahman and Weston, say he is optimistic about Bangladesh?

3. According to Manning, as quoted by the authors, why did Henry Ford pay his workers double the going rate?

*T*he Daily Star *caught up with Alan Manning, a London School of Economics (LSE) professor, at a reception hosted by the alumni association of LSE in Bangladesh. Alan, who has published extensively on UK minimum wage, unemployment and related labour issues, was in Dhaka for a week with his Bangladesh-born wife and their children. Our nation has struggled for years to set acceptable wages in the apparel industry, the country's largest manufacturing sector. He was aware of this, but has not studied it, and so agreed to answer more general questions about national minimum wages and their effects around the world.*

In Favor of Minimum Wage

"I am generally in favour of a minimum wage, even in Bangladesh," said Manning, the head of the LSE economics department. But he questioned Bangladesh's ability to enforce it. "The problem is with its enforcement: If you are going to have it, you have to enforce it."

Manning cited the experience of Latin American countries as a cautionary tale. Many set a minimum wage without an ability to enforce it in at least half the economy, often referred to as informal because it does not register with or pay taxes to the state. "You basically create a very unequal playing field," because "you're putting an unfair burden on those [employers] who comply."

The LSE professor also said the first minimum wage level must first be set near the lowest level of wages paid in that economy prior to the law. "Everything depends on the level at which a country sets it," Manning said. "A poor country's wage floor must reflect its economy. The wage will differ country to country on the basis of supply and demand of workers and their skills. If you set it too high, you're going to price people out of jobs."

The economist called the recent labour unrest in many countries, including Bangladesh, a common phenomenon. "That's natural; they (workers) want to get a better life," he said. But the minimum wage must be "looked at from both the perspective of employees and from the company's profitability."

That means private sector workers and managers must succeed in increasing productivity together if the minimum wage is to rise in a competitive industry or they will both fail together. "If you cannot get your productivity up [. . .] then you are out of a job," the economist said.

Many developing countries have surplus workers who are therefore holding the short stick in the balance of power between labour and capital, he noted: "Trade unions can play an important role, but again, it is a balance of supply and demand of workers."

No Job Losses

"Obviously, in the south [i.e., the Southern Hemisphere], problems sometimes get worse before they get better," he said. But he is "optimistic" about Bangladesh's prospects, saying that it impresses him with its "dynamism".

The noted economist was a member of the UK Minimum Wage Council, which was first introduced by Winston Churchill in 1909 in specific sectors only. His study found that enforcing minimum wage in the UK did not cause any job losses. The minimum wage was abolished in 1993, but [prime minister] Tony Blair's government reintroduced it in 1999.

Raising a minimum wage in developed economies most often does not produce the job losses that conservative economists expect, his studies found. "Everybody looks at the minimum wage from the perspective of the employers. It obviously makes labour more expensive, and so they might reduce the amount of labour they employ."

But employers have other important costs related to labour that are not as obvious, such as high turnover in low-paying jobs, which is reduced when minimum wages rise. He cites the example of auto pioneer Henry Ford, who in 1914 started to pay his workers $5 day—double the going rate—for shorter hours. "He did that because he had a problem with incredibly high turnover rate; he would get the workers trained up, they left [due to the dullness of assembly-line work] and he actually felt it was more efficient to pay higher wages.

A higher wage floor draws more and better people into the workforce. It also often increases their productivity, as owners have a stronger incentive to buy labour-saving equipment or tweak their output, the economist explained. "Wage can increase the productivity and supply of workers as well," he said. "What you often see, such as in France, [is that] the employers make a lot of fuss about how they're all going to go bust because of this [new higher wage], but then, after a bit, nothing much happens."

Manning said trade unions can play a cooperative role if they are free, but this is not always the case, particularly in the least developed economies: "It is a global problem that unions may not represent the real interests of workers." He supports freely elected union leaders, but notes that it does not guarantee responsive leadership, even in developed countries. "It's a problem in many countries that the trade unions may not represent the workers. It becomes empire-building within the union leadership," he says, which makes unionisation less attractive to non-workers.

The professor also urged the Bangladeshi students heading for the LSE this year to profit from the opportunity of studying in LSE, with its diverse mix of international students, which now includes more from China than any other country.

Periodical and Internet Sources Bibliography

The following articles have been selected to supplement the diverse views presented in this chapter.

Fiona Anderson	"Ireland, Minimum Wage and HST," *Vancouver Sun* (Canada), November 25, 2010.
Australian Broadcasting Corporation News	"Opinion Split over Minimum Wage Rise," June 3, 2010. www.abc .net.au.
BBC News	"Bangladesh Increases Garment Workers' Minimum Wage," July 27, 2010. www.bbc.co.uk.
China Post	"China Ups Minimum Wage as Inflation Persists," January 27, 2011. www.chinapost.com.
Jeff Groat	"Opinion: Increasing Minimum Wage Makes Sense," *Kwantlen Polytechnic University Chronicle*, October 12, 2010.
Ewin Hannan	"Minimum Pay Rise Dangerous for Small Business, Bosses," *Australian*, June 3, 2010.
Amanda Kloer	"Bangladesh Increases Minimum Wage Despite Walmart's Obstruction," Change.org, November 6, 2010. http://news .change.org.
Luo Xi and Xue Li	"China's Minimum Wage One of the Lowest in the World," *Epoch Times*, February 26, 2010.
Racehel Pannett	"Australia Raises Minimum Wage," *Wall Street Journal*, June 3, 2010.
Reuters	"IMF Urges Ireland to Cut Jobless Pay, Minimum Wage," November 23, 2010. http://in.reuters.com.
Jim Sinclair	"Premier's Minimum Wage Hike Booed, Applauded," *Vancouver Sun* (Canada), March 22, 2011.

For Further Discussion

Chapter 1

1. Wayne Lusvardi compares the minimum wage in California to a winning lottery ticket. Does that comparison seem fair? Would Kai Filion and James Sherk agree with Lusvardi? Explain.

2. William E. Spriggs argues that a low minimum wage has historically hurt women and minorities. Compare this with the viewpoint by Rahn and Santa. Which viewpoint makes the more convincing case? Cite evidence from each viewpoint in your answer.

Chapter 2

1. The viewpoint by Business for a Fair Minimum Wage quotes many business owners in favor of a minimum wage hike. What reasons do the business owners give for wanting a minimum wage increase? Based on the viewpoint by Timothy P. Carney, what reasons might some business owners have for supporting a minimum wage increase that they might not be willing to state publically?

2. Laurence M. Vance and Stephen Herrington both argue that the minimum wage has serious ethical implications. Do either of them make a convincing case? Do you think they are overstating or understating the moral issues at stake? Explain your answers.

Chapter 3

1. Based on the viewpoints by Ivan Light and David R. Henderson, could a stronger enforcement of the minimum wage reduce illegal immigration? Is effective stronger enforcement plausible or likely? Why or why not?

2. Of the writers in this chapter, which think that illegal immigration is a serious problem and which do not? Whom do you find most convincing? Why?

Chapter 4

1. In light of the first four viewpoints, are the arguments around minimum wage in Canada and Australia similar to arguments in the United States? Explain and identify any differences in the debates.

2. In Egypt, failure to raise the minimum wage was linked to social unrest; in China the minimum wage was raised to prevent social unrest. Do you think that eliminating the minimum wage in the United States would lead to social unrest? Explain.

Organizations to Contact

The editors have compiled the following list of organizations concerned with the issues debated in this book. The descriptions are derived from materials provided by the organizations. All have publications or information available for interested readers. The list was compiled on the date of publication of the present volume; names, addresses, phone and fax numbers, and e-mail and Internet addresses may change. Be aware that many organizations take several weeks or longer to respond to inquiries, so allow as much time as possible.

Business for Shared Prosperity
PO Box 301045
Boston, MA 02130
(617) 522-2923
e-mail: info@businessforsharedprosperity.org
website: www.businessforsharedprosperity.org

Business for Shared Property is a network of business owners, executives, and investors committed to building economic progress on a foundation of opportunity, equity, and innovation. It supports public policies that expand economic opportunity and reduce inequality. One of its projects is Business for a Fair Minimum Wage, which uses the media to advocate for increases in the minimum wage. Its website includes press releases, news bulletins, and other resources.

Cato Institute
1000 Massachusetts Ave. NW
Washington, DC 20001-5403
(202) 842-0200 • fax: (202) 842-3490
website: www.cato.org

The Cato Institute is a libertarian public policy research foundation dedicated to increasing the understanding of public policies based on the principles of limited government, free markets, individual liberty, and peace. It publishes the *Cato Journal* three times a year, the periodic *Cato Policy Analysis*, and a bimonthly newsletter, *Cato Policy Review*. The website also includes articles such as "The Economics of Minimum Wage Legislation Revisited" and "Below the Minimum Wage."

Center for American Progress (CAP)
1333 H St. NW, 10th Fl.
Washington, DC 20005
(202) 682-1611 • fax: (202) 682-1867
e-mail: progress@americanprogress.org
website: www.americanprogress.org

Founded in 2003, the Center for American Progress is a progressive think tank that researches, formulates, and advocates for a bold, progressive public policy agenda. CAP supports affirmative action and the minimum wage. The CAP website posts numerous webpages and publications, including "State of the Minimum Wage" and "Time for National Change on Minimum Wage."

Center for Immigration Studies (CIS)
1522 K St. NW, Ste. 820
Washington, DC 20005-1202
(202) 466-8185 • fax: (202) 466-8076
e-mail: center@cis.org
website: www.cis.org

The Center for Immigration Studies is an independent nonpartisan, nonprofit research organization. It provides immigration policy makers, the academic community, news media, and concerned citizens with information about the social, economic, environmental, security, and fiscal consequences of legal and illegal immigration to the United States. The CIS website includes op-eds, reports, publications, court testimony, and other resources, many of which discuss the relationship between minimum wage and immigration.

Economic Policy Institute

1333 H St. NW, Ste. 300, East Tower
Washington, DC 20005-4707
(202) 775-8810 • fax: (202) 775-0819
e-mail: researchdept@epi.org
website: http://www.epi.org

The Economic Policy Institute is a nonprofit Washington think tank that focuses on the economic policy interests of low- and middle-income workers. It conducts research, publishes studies and books, briefs policy makers, provides support to activists, and provides information to the media and public. Its website includes research reports, news reports, issue briefs, and more, including a "Minimum Wage Issue Guide."

Employment Policies Institute (EPI)

1090 Vermont Ave. NW, Ste. 800
Washington, DC 20005
(202) 463-7650 ext. 109 • fax: (202) 463-7107
e-mail: info@epionline.org
website: http://epionline.org

The Employment Policies Institute is a nonprofit research organization dedicated to studying public policy issues surrounding employment growth. In particular, EPI focuses on issues that affect entry-level employment. Much of its research focuses on the harm done by the minimum wage. Papers on its website include "Failed Stimulus: Minimum Wage Increases and Their Failure to Boost Gross Domestic Product" and "Unequal Harm: Racial Disparities in the Employment Consequences of Minimum Wage Increases."

The Heritage Foundation

214 Massachusetts Ave. NE
Washington, DC 20002
(202) 546-4400 • fax: (202) 546-8328
e-mail: info@heritage.org

website: www.heritage.org

The Heritage Foundation is a conservative public policy research institute dedicated to the principles of free, competitive enterprise, limited government, and individual liberty. Its scholars write numerous articles on politics and the economy. Among its publications are the periodic *Backgrounder* series and its website also includes numerous articles and policy position papers, including "Econ 101: The Minimum Wage Kills Jobs" and "The Economic Effects of the Minimum Wage."

National Employment Law Project (NELP)
75 Maiden Ln., Ste. 601
New York, NY 10038
(212) 285-3025 • fax: (212) 285-3044
website: www.nelp.org

The National Employment Law Project works to restore the promise of economic opportunity to American workers by promoting policies and programs that create good jobs, strengthen upward mobility, enforce worker rights, and help unemployed workers regain their economic footing. Its activities include research, technical assistance for advocates, bringing together coalitions, and providing public education through media outreach. NELP is committed to the minimum wage, and its website includes articles such as "Minimum Wage Doesn't Kill Jobs" and "Study Underscores Positive Role of Minimum Wage Increases."

United States Bureau of Labor Statistics
Postal Square Bldg.,
2 Massachusetts Ave. NE
Washington, DC 20212-0001
(202) 691-5200 • TDD: (800) 877-8339
website: www.bls.gov

The Bureau of Labor Statistics is the principal fact-finding agency for the federal government in the field of labor economics and statistics. It publishes a range of publications, including *Monthly Labor Review* (downloadable) and the *Editor's Desk*, a daily updated online feature. Its website includes many articles and publications about the minimum wage.

United States Department of Labor
200 Constitution Ave. NW
Washington, DC 20210
(866) 4-USA-DOL (487-2365) • TTY: (877) 889-5627
website: www.dol.gov

The Department of Labor is the United States Cabinet-level agency responsible for occupational safety, wage and hour standards, unemployment insurance benefits, reemployment services, and some economics statistics. Its website includes numerous articles and reports on the minimum wage.

Bibliography of Books

Piroleau Alexander

You Want Fries with That? A White-Collar Burnout Experiences Life at Minimum Wage. New York: Arcade, 2008.

Kim Bobo

Wage Theft in America: Why Millions of Working Americans Are Not Getting Paid—and What We Can Do About It. New York: New Press, 2009.

Ronald C. Brown

Understanding Labor and Employment Law in China. New York: Cambridge University Press, 2010.

Aviva Chomsky

"They Take Our Jobs!": And 20 Other Myths About Immigration. Boston: Beacon, 2007.

Wendy V. Cunningham

Minimum Wages and Social Policy: Lessons from Developing Countries. Washington DC: The International Bank for Reconstruction and Development, 2007.

Christian Dustmann and Albrecht Glitz

Immigration, Jobs and Wages: Theory, Evidence and Opinion. London: Center for Economic Policy Research, 2005.

Barbara Ehrenreich

Nickel and Dimed: On (Not) Getting By in America. New York: Henry Holt, 2001.

Jeff Faux

The Global Class War: How America's Bipartisan Elite Lost Our Future—and What It Will Take to Win It Back. Hoboken, NJ: Wiley, 2006.

Charles Fishman

The Wal-Mart Effect: How the World's Most Powerful Company Really Works—and How It's Transforming the American Economy. New York: Penguin, 2006.

Jerome Gautie and John Schmitt, eds.

Low-Wage Work in the Wealthy World. New York: Russell Sage, 2010.

Daniel P. Glitterman

Boosting Paychecks: The Politics of Supporting America's Working Poor. Washington, DC: Brookings, 2010.

Alice Kessler-Harris

A Woman's Wage: Historical Meanings and Social Consequences. Lexington: University Press of Kentucky, 1990.

Mark Krikorian

The New Case Against Immigration: Both Legal and Illegal. New York: Sentinel, 2008.

Oren M. Levin-Waldman

The Case of the Minimum Wage: Competing Policy Models. Albany: State University of New York Press, 2001.

Helen Masterman-Smith and Barbara Pocock

Living Low Paid: The Dark Side of Prosperous Australia. St. Leonards, NSW, Australia: Allen & Unwin, 2008.

| David Neumark and William L. Wascher | *Minimum Wages.* Cambridge, MA: MIT Press, 2008. |

| Margaret O'Brien-Strain and Thomas E. Macurdy | *Increasing the Minimum Wage: California's Winners and Losers.* San Francisco: Public Policy Institute of California, 2000. |

| Robert Pollin, Mark Brenner, Jeannette Wicks-Lim, and Stephanie Luce | *A Measure of Fairness: The Economics of Living Wages and Minimum Wages.* Ithaca, NY: Cornell University Press, 2008. |

| Steven Shulman, ed. | *The Impact of Immigration on African Americans.* Piscataway, NJ: Transaction, 2004. |

| Holly Sklar, Laryssa Mykyta, and Susan Wefald | *Raise the Floor: Wages and Policies That Work for All of Us.* Boston: South End, 2001. |

| Carol M. Swain | *Debating Immigration.* New York: Cambridge University Press, 2007. |

| Gabriel Thompson | *Working in the Shadows: A Year of Doing the Jobs (Most) Americans Won't Do.* New York: Perseus, 2010. |

| Daniel Vaughn-Whitehead | *The Minimum Wage Revisited in the Enlarged EU.* Geneva, Switzerland: International Labour Office, 2010. |

| Jerold L. Waltman | *The Case for the Living Wage.* New York: Algora, 2004. |

| Jerold L. Waltman | *Minimum Wage Policy in Great Britain and the United States.* New York: Algora, 2008. |

Index